Cohabiting WITH COMPUTERS

Cohabiting WITH COMPUTERS

JOSEPH F. TRAUB, EDITOR

with chapters by

GORDON BELL

JOEL S. BIRNBAUM

LEWIS M. BRANSCOMB

EDWARD E. DAVID, JR.

PETER LIKINS

WILLIAM F. MILLER

ARNO PENZIAS

HERBERT A. SIMON

ROBERT SPINRAD

JOSEPH F. TRAUB

William Kaufmann, Inc.
Los Altos, California

10 9 8 7 6 5 4 3 2 1

Printed in the United States of America

Library of Congress Cataloging in Publication Data

Main entry under title:

Cohabiting with computers.

  Includes index.
    1. Computers—Addresses, essays, lectures.
2. Computers and civilization—Addresses, essays,
lectures. I. Traub, J. F. (Joseph Frederick), 1932–
QA76.24.C64 1984   303.49834   84-27768
ISBN 0-86576-079-9

Contents

Preface

Books about computers, their evolution, their operations, their future development, and their effects on our lives abound. But few of them are both entertaining and informative, and even fewer combine these qualities with the authority and richness of content that will be immediately apparent to the readers of this slender volume.

No one today can keep up with the floods of literature in various forms—books, magazines, journals, manuals, seminars, tutorials, audio-visual cassettes, on-line sources, and so on—that purport to tell us all about modern computers and the accelerating, electronics-driven, high tech revolution in communications and information systems.

Of course most of us do not need to be up-to-the-minute on all such matters. And, fortunately for us, insofar as we do there are occasional books or timely critical reviews of large areas of interest that come to our rescue. Books such as this one bring together in readable and readily digestible form creative syntheses of vast amounts of interesting and

important information that is often scattered through the
pages of occasional publications, technical reports, professional journals, and other hard-to-track sources. Tremendous amounts of time and effort would be required for any
lay reader or even for most experts merely to find it all, let
alone try to read and understand it.

Each chapter in *Cohabiting with Computers* represents a
creative synthesis in which the author addresses in detail
some of the issues and dilemmas we face in "cohabiting the
planet with computers,"—a prospect that is not a distant
one by any means, since people are already outnumbered
by computers on our crowded planet. The long term effects
of the explosive growth of computers on our life-styles,
work habits, social relations, and a host of other aspects of
modern living are far from clear in these dawning years of
the computer age, but the trends noted and the opportunities, problems, and challenges addressed in these pages are
of enormous import for all of us.

Creators of new knowledge, that is to say people like the
authors of the chapters in this volume, carry on their work
in universities, corporations, and other types of research
environments all over the world. Great researchers/leaders,
of the kind represented here, are uncommon, as are the outstanding synthesizers (sometimes the selfsame individuals) who can consume, absorb, retain, and distill out for
the benefit of others the essential insights and possible
implications of theoretical and applied research and development as it progresses in their chosen fields. Luckily for
most of us, lectures, articles, and books by these exceptional
leaders permit us relatively safe and easy access into the
narrowest corridors of scientific research and allow us fascinating glimpses into the new frontiers for the human brain
and the coevolution of its fascinating new electronic counterparts.

It was the dedication of a new computer science building
at the Columbia University Convocation held October
10–11, 1983 that provided the occasion for bringing together
a group of fine original thinkers, researchers, scholars, and
synthesizers in computer science—this relatively new

academic discipline, which came into being only a scant two decades ago. The ten chapters in this book are based upon the public addresses presented on that occasion. The Convocation culminated in the conferral of the honorary degree of Doctor of Science, *honoris causa,* on Herbert A. Simon, from whom so many have learned so much. The citation for his degree appears on page 154, and his evocative chapter provides a fitting conclusion to this book.

The book as a whole sketches in broad outlines the possible future directions of our educational-industrial-societal complex, touching as well on the age-old questions of human destiny and the search of individuals for personal fulfillment. Topics such as computer consciousness, the value of information, knowledge as power, information as a basic resource, and fifth-generation computing, move toward the center of contemporary thought and dialog. As individuals, groups, and institutions attempt to come to grips with the problems and issues of the day, these concepts will surely increasingly occupy the best minds of present and future generations. Recurring themes throughout this book are the challenges we face with a growing sense of urgency in the closing years of the 20th century.

John Naisbitt, social analyst and author of the widely read 1982 book called *Megatrends,* has observed, "In times of great changes, the individual's power and leverage are enormous. . . . We can either become victims of the great changes coming—or we can make them work for us to accomplish extraordinary things." One by one, many people—as individuals, families, and even as nations— discover (or rediscover) the truth that opportunities can be made or found in every new generation. The ideas, insights, and predictions offered to perceptive readers of this book will stimulate creative thought and perhaps even positive action: highly motivated readers may well be provoked to try to make their own significant contributions in tomorrow's world and to find their own prominent places in the unfolding scheme of things.

Specific bibliographic citations and references have not

been provided for most of the chapters, because this is not intended to be an academic treatise, but rather a book for lay readers. However, those who are stimulated to seek further details can find additional material in local newsstands, bookstores, and libraries. The outpouring of new publications continues, and the pace of publication makes any listing of related references in a book such as this quickly obsolescent in computer science and related fields. Furthermore, computerized information retrieval makes it a relatively easy matter for interested readers to find up-to-the-minute references by accessing the many databases available to libraries or individuals with their own computer terminals and networks.

The Convocation required great efforts by dedicated people at Columbia. I am particularly grateful to Robert Dunne, Kerny McLaughlin, and Margaret Montana.

On behalf of my colleagues at Columbia University, the sponsors and attendees of the Convocation, and our readers, I am delighted to extend our warmest thanks to the speakers whose creative contributions have made this book possible.

Joseph F. Traub, Editor

1. Perspectives on a High-Tech Society

WILLIAM F. MILLER

1. Perspectives on a High-Tech Society

WILLIAM F. MILLER

No mere technological optimist, Dr. Miller foresees a period of dynamic cultural and economic change and revitalization ahead for America. The basic tools of this transformation will be high technology and venture capital, powered by entrepreneurial activity and fundamental changes in American values.

TODAY I would like to share with you nine perspectives on the future environment, in particular on the environment for a high-tech society.

By perspectives I mean something like the scenarios that the futurists use, but I do not like the word scenario because it implies a truly worked out hypothesis about what the future might be. In my view, scenarios contain too much detail and too much thought about the fine interactions in a computerized model. Getting into too much detail defeats the purpose of thinking about the future. This is a question not only of seeing the trees instead of the forest but also of failing to see trees that have not yet sprouted. Or failing to notice that "the forest" might not be a useful concept if you're looking at a tree farm.

We'd be better off considering "frameworks for thinking

about the future." We all operate with certain mental maps, or sets of assumptions about the world. When these maps are wrong, the consequences can be disastrous.

For example, consider the "Singapore mentality" of the British military leaders of the 1930s. They built Singapore as the bastion of their defense system in the Far East, and armed it with long-range artillery pieces more powerful than any guns that could be carried on ships. They succeeded in making Singapore an impregnable fortress— from the sea. The British mental map, their strategic assumption, did not envision foot soldiers working their way down through the supposedly impenetrable jungles of the Malaysian peninsula. When the Japanese did precisely this, the defenders of Singapore found they couldn't turn their powerful artillery pieces around because the guns were set in massive concrete embankments facing the sea. Singapore fell without a struggle because the military planners were operating on a set of fundamentally wrong assumptions.

When we look at the world from useful and relevant perspectives, on the other hand, we will not be totally surprised. We gain a greater measure of control over our future.

Of course, the future will contain genuine surprises— what futurists call "wild cards." For example, who could possibly have predicted that the Soviets would shoot down a Korean jetliner, an act with profound consequences both for world opinion of the Soviets and for the Soviet system itself? Who can predict when an assassination may change the course of a nation, or of the world?

A theme of individualism runs through the nine perspectives I will discuss—not the selfish individualism that gave rise to colonialism and robber barons, but individualism inwardly directed toward self-reliance and self-satisfaction.

1. The Crisis of Complex Institutions

In the United States and many other countries today we face a growing tendency toward what we might call "institutional deadlock." Our giant institutions have been under increasing attack for nearly two decades. The legitimacy of

big government, big business, big unions, educational institutions, traditional churches, and so on has been chal-
lenged.

We are all familiar with the growing inefficiency of, and
our disenchantment with, big government. Many people
believe, as an eminent historian wrote, that "Governments
can do only two things well: wage war and inflate the currency." This disenchantment elected Ronald Reagan, who
ran against big government, and it may reelect him in 1984,
the year when George Orwell prophesied the dominion of
"Big Brother."

Big business, too, has taken its lumps. Let me give you a
concrete example: From 1970 to 1982, the United States
added 25 million new jobs to the work force, an impressive
achievement. But a deeper look reveals that the Fortune 500
companies, as a group, added no net jobs during this
period. The net new jobs were created in smaller
companies—about 60 percent of them in very small, high-
technology companies.

A similar phenomenon, a loss of performance, is evident
in other giant institutions, including the unions and the traditional churches. They are in negative-growth or low-
growth situations today.

2. Decentralization, and the Growth of
   Single-Issue Politics

Five years ago, a senior consultant at SRI was advising a
large utility in the southwestern United States. The management of the utility realized that the increasing cost of
energy and especially the deregulation of natural gas created a public relations problem for them that could seriously constrain their ability to operate. They called in a
leading public relations firm. Instead of asking the firm to
help them identify the opinion leaders in their markets,
they asked it to find out who influenced the opinion leaders
and how these leaders were forming their opinions.

The answer was unambiguous. The opinion leaders were
listening to the single-issue groups—the environmentalists,
the anti-oil-industry activists, the antinuclear movement,

and the consumer action groups, to name just a few.

In our American democracy, government requires the consent of the governed—especially the consensus consent of the governed. But in the United States today no consensus exists; instead hundreds of single-issue groups pound on the doors of congressional cloakrooms and on the doors of the constituents at home. Many such groups have what amounts to a "hit list." They will attempt to terminate the political future of any legislator who votes against them.

The impact of this erosion of consensus upon our political system is profound. Contending single-issue groups have arisen around virtually every important issue you can name. Someone is likely to confront each legislator with a well-orchestrated, well-financed and deadly serious campaign whenever he or she is due to vote on an important issue. More than any other factor, single-issue groups have contributed to the increasing paralysis of the United States Congress and, indeed, of our entire political system. Why? Because single-issue groups have great power to stop things from happening but far less power to make things happen.

If our giant institutions are increasingly paralyzed, what *is* working in America today? A lot, including our creative local problem-solving initiatives.

3. The Grass Roots Revolution in Local Initiatives

For the past five years, Americans have been increasingly disenchanted with reliance upon the federal government to solve local problems. Even before the current administration took office, many communities had realized that the way to address urgent local needs was to mobilize the constituents with a direct stake in the issue. These communities found that money alone would not necessarily solve local problems. Money is, after all, only one form of energy. Other, more important forms of energy can be harnessed at the local level, including management expertise, local volunteer organizations, and, above all, the powers of local governments to set and/or modify policies and regulations. At SRI, we have assembled over 1,000 case histories of local communities that have set such public/private initiatives in motion.

Such efforts have been especially successful in five areas:

- Housing and community development
- Education and training
- Human services
- Public services and facilities
- Economic development and job creation

Here is what typically happens. A local community decides to mobilize its energy and other resources, often under the leadership of a business or a group of businesses. In doing so, it somehow draws together everyone who has a stake in the problem or its solution.

Often the issue is specific—e.g. summer jobs for students, day care for the children of working parents, low-income housing, or care for the elderly. By getting all the stakeholders to commit themselves to solving the problem, communities find that significant obstacles can suddenly be overcome.

For example, have you ever tried to get a building code, a zoning regulation, or a licensing procedure changed? In ordinary circumstances, these are impossible goals. But when the key stakeholders organize for change, these immutable "rules" by which we operate can suddenly be modified quite easily.

We see another example of local initiative in education. Many corporations lend the expertise of executives and technical specialists to public schools. Others donate the use of corporate computer facilities and high-technology equipment for student training. Still others provide advice to school administrators on new technologies and management techniques.

In other cases, corporations alter their work rules to allow after-school work, half-time work, and flex-time schedules. They undertake affirmative hiring programs for women, the elderly, or the handicapped. They develop special training programs for people on welfare, for refugees, or for minority groups. They provide on-site work experience programs for high-school students. Companies coordinate their in-company training programs with public education programs.

This public-private approach to community problem solving has caught on so well that United Way of America is creating a special program to help facilitate community problem solving in the human services area.

An excellent SRI document outlines a number of these public/private problem-solving initiatives. It's called "In Good Company."

4. The Revolution in Values

The industrialized world is undergoing a fundamental change in values—something as profound as the values revolution that took place between the Middle Ages and the Renaissance. Historian Louis Mumford has an interesting way of describing the magnitude of that change. According to Mumford, six of the Seven Deadly Sins of the Middle Ages—pride, avarice, lust, gluttony, envy, and rage (aggressiveness or competitiveness)—became virtues that powered the Renaissance and later the Industrial Revolution. Competitive, ambitious, acquisitive, materialistic values spurred people on to do, to create, to achieve, to want, and to acquire. These same values, in various forms, are behind the main advertising appeals that have worked well through recent decades. Where would Madison Avenue be if its ads couldn't exploit pride, avarice, lust, gluttony, envy, and competitiveness?

Today, however, many people are turning away from materialism. They are turning away from loyalty to the old institutions. They are turning away from the nationalism of "my country, right or wrong." The generation that emerged from schools and universities in the 1960s has experienced what its members call "the poverty of affluence." Now these individuals, whom I will call "new-values people," prefer a life that is, in their words, "outwardly more simple and inwardly more rich." Such people have had a revolutionary impact on society. They make up less than 25% of the population; but they are well-educated people who know how to manipulate the system—how to make their views count. It was they who set the social agenda of the United States in the 1960s and 1970s.

They have a commitment to issues like world peace, protecting the environment, social welfare, corporate responsibility, holistic health, affirmative action, and women's rights. They spur the growth of single-issue politics. And their impact on life in America is only beginning.

Their impact on corporate management is also only beginning. Inner-directed employees do not respond to the traditional carrots and sticks. For example, they will not readily relocate themselves and their families in exchange for a promotion and a handsome salary increase. They are not "loyal employees" in the old sense. They do not believe that what is right for General Motors is necessarily right for the nation. They do not put the company first and their individual fulfillment second. Yet corporations need their talents.

For corporations that want to attract the best and brightest of current college students who hold such values, I have dismaying news. When I recently asked my students at the Stanford Business School whether they intended to work in large corporations, only a few said yes. Why didn't more have such a goal? They did not believe that large corporations provided personally rewarding jobs, a real career challenge, or a corporate climate in which they wanted to work. Instead, my students wanted to make their marks in smaller, more entrepreneurial companies.

A widespread misunderstanding has arisen concerning these new-values people. Contrary to what many critics assume, they are not turning away from the traditional work ethic upon which America was built. When Arnold Mitchell initiated our Values and Lifestyle Program at SRI in 1978, he tested this hypothesis by means of extensive nationwide surveys. There is every indication that the new-values, or inner-directed, people work as hard as traditional employees who believe in "an honest day's pay for an honest day's work." Our management experience at SRI confirms Arnold's survey findings.

As the United States shifts from being an industrial society to being an information society, we will be dealing more and more with this new set of values. This is a very large challenge. If we meet it, the creative vitality of our business system will be preserved.

5. The Information Society as a Model for Employment

The United States is being transformed from an industrial society to an information society. We are moving from a capital-intensive labor- and resource-based economy to one based on services, and on the information and electronic technologies. In fact, information and human resources are becoming the key strategic resources, even more important than land and capital.

Information is a strange resource, very different from what we are used to dealing with in our industrial society. Unlike land, capital, and labor, information is very difficult to price. We don't know what information is worth. Bad information may be worth zero or less, but the value of vital information may be inestimable. In the hands of the right person, in the right place, at the right time, information may be powerful; to someone who doesn't know how to use it, the same information may be virtually useless.

We are already quite far along in the transition from the industrial society to the information society. Only about one third of the U.S. work force is employed in the manufacturing sector, and only 13% in production-line jobs. More than two thirds of our workers are currently employed in information-based jobs, according to a recent Commerce Department study.

What is an information society like? I suggest that California is the best precursor or model for the coming information society. It is not a perfect model but it may be the best one we have. If California were a nation, it would have the sixth largest GNP in the world. Its economy is based upon information services, agriculture, aerospace, forest products, electronics, financial services, and various retail and wholesale services. Each of these sectors in turn involves electronics and information technologies. California manufacturers concentrate on the high-technology end of the aerospace business, for example—communication systems, guidance systems, electronic countermeasure systems, and so on. California agriculture is becoming a high-technology business, where sophisticated farming operations rely on computers as well as fertilizers and pesticides. California agribusinesses are among the more sophisticated users of computerized cash flow management. They also use computers for crop and livestock planning. In the manufacture of California's forest products, the old lumber mill has given way to sophisticated cellulose conversion processing plants—highly automated and computerized. Finally, breakthroughs in data processing, telecommunications and microelectronics have allowed California banks to offer new financial services at unprecedented rates. In fact, "bank" is an obsolete word: "diversified financial services institution" is a more accurate descriptor.

Let us look at the years 1973–1980 in California as a baseline era. During each year from 1973 to 1980 California added nearly 500,000 new jobs, net, to its work force, which in 1980 numbered about 10 million people out of a population of about 22 million. (This employment rate alone is impressive; nearly half of the state's population is working, which means that virtually everyone of working age had access to a job during the period under consideration.)

Of the half million new jobs that were added, net, in California, each year from 1973 to 1980, something like 60% were created directly or indirectly by the new technologies. (Interestingly, few were created in the electronics-computer-telecommunications industry itself, where there are no more than 300,000–400,000 jobs, depending on how broadly you define it. It grew very rapidly during this period, but the total number of jobs remained relatively small.) The job growth occurred in the industries using the new information technologies. We can call this "the ripple effect."

I can provide two striking examples: First, Pacific Telephone—one of the most highly automated and techno-logically sophisticated companies in the world—doubled its size and became the largest employer in the state during this period, with about 100,000 employees by 1980. Reason: the new communications technologies allowed PacTel, growing at better than 10% per year, to create new services for its customers, and thus new jobs, faster than old jobs (e.g. telephone operator) were automated out of existence.

The second example concerns the banking industry, or rather the financial services industry, because deregulation and the impact of the new information technologies have virtually eliminated the borderline between banking and other financial services. California has become the financial services capital for the Pacific Basin, which is the fastest growing economic region in the world. The trade flow across the Pacific is already greater than that across the Atlantic.

When computers were first introduced into banking 20 years ago, many predicted that they would eliminate jobs in that industry. Precisely the opposite has happened. Since 1973 banking has grown at better than 10% per year—again, because the new technologies allowed the banks to offer new services to their customers and serve new classes of customers, creating new jobs faster than traditional paper-handling jobs were eliminated.

Let's look briefly at California's manufacturing activities.

From 1973 to 1980, consumer income went up an average of about 12% per year. Yet, value added in manufacturing went up by about 18% per year. The difference between these two rates represents the creation of new wealth and new capital. And indeed, today California is virtually awash in a new and exciting form of capital—venture capital (see below).

The California model indicates that the information tech-nologies are job-creating, not job-destroying. This has been true of all past technologies, throughout history. And as in the past, so today, new technologies tend to produce dislocations and painful adjustments during the transitional stages.

To sum up, the ripple effect of the new information technologies has benefited many sectors of the "nation" of California—diversified light manufacturing enterprises, retail and wholesale stores, financial and other services, real estate values, and the tax rolls, to mention only a few.

The problem in California is not whether there will be enough jobs to occupy our people but, rather, whether we can find enough technically trained people to fill the jobs. Our problem, in short, is the mismatch between our traditional, production-oriented work force and the new information jobs that are being created.

Indeed, since 1970, the United States as a nation has created more new jobs than ever before in history. The work force has expanded from 75 million in 1970 to 104.2 million in 1984—an addition of nearly 30 million jobs. This is an achievement without parallel in economic history. And the vast majority of these new jobs were information jobs (only 2.3 million were manufacturing jobs).

We are seeing the growth of "high-tech" centers in parts of the nation other than California—for example, the area around Route 128 in Massachusetts and the Research Triangle in North Carolina. Tennessee has detailed plans for the development of a "Technology Corridor" in the Oakridge-Knoxville area. Similar developments are occurring in Texas, Michigan, Minnesota, Arizona, Colorado, Washington, and Georgia, to mention only a few.

All these high-tech centers bring together the capital resources, the industrial or manufacturing resources, and above all, the educational or human resources required to support the new information and electronic industries. They are also becoming international high-tech centers, attracting foreign companies that wish to position themselves to compete in the U.S. market.

Based on the California Model, it seems likely that the information technologies can create new jobs at an unprecedented rate. We at SRI suggest that the traditional "S-curve" of economic development will change its slope in the 1980s.

Up to now, many developmental economists have believed that the industrial world has reached the top of the S-curve; that the rate of increase in productivity will continue to taper off, as it has been doing since the Golden Economic Era of the 1950s and 1960s. At SRI, however, we believe that the new information technologies—especially factory and office automation—will extend and steepen the shape of the S-curve. We believe that there will be a new burst of productivity (see below), and that the impacts of these new technologies will start to be felt in the second half of this decade and reach very high levels by the end of the decade.

6. The Emerging Technologies of the 1980s

Five technologies will be driving forces in the next decade:

- Information Technology
- New Materials
- Factory and Office Automation
- Biotechnology
- Health and Medical Technologies

Human beings have two characteristics that determine the pace of technological development. Man is a tool maker—a maker of technologies—and man is a social being—a maker of organizations. There has always been an interplay between our technologies and our social organizations. In some cases, there is a pull—a demand from society for new technologies; in other cases, new technologies push themselves into society, opening up new opportunities. Today, in the United States and worldwide, both tendencies are at work. The changing availability of natural resources and global competition generate a demand for new technologies. The creation of entirely new technologies and products opens up new human vistas.

Today, the pace of innovation and the rate of introduction of new technologies are continuing to increase. Four factors are contributing to what will be a virtual explosion of new technologies in the 1980s and 1990s.

First, the seeds of scientific research planted after World War II are now bearing fruit. The technologies being commercialized today are a direct outgrowth of that research. (Most of the new technologies introduced in the 1960s and 1970s were an outgrowth of scientific research that started before World War II.) Not only did this post-World War II impulse produce new scientific ideas; it also produced a rapid increase in the supply of scientifically and technically trained manpower, and of managers who are comfortable directing the introduction of new technologies.

Second, global competition and the worldwide demand for new products have stimulated major efforts by industry to capitalize on new scientific ideas. In addition to introducing products that permit new levels of performance or provide new capabilities, companies are giving special emphasis to technologies that conserve energy and scarce materials and enhance human performance.

The third factor contributing to the explosion of new technologies is the increasing availability of venture capital and other forms of high-risk investment money to support and stimulate embryonic high-technology companies.

The fourth factor is a wave of entrepreneurship more extensive than any we have experienced in the past. Back in 1950 some 93,000 new companies were incorporated in the United States. In 1981 and 1982—despite the recession and the unprecedentedly high cost of money—some 550,000 new incorporations were formed each year. We at SRI estimate that more than 600,000 new companies will be formed in 1984. The marriage of the venture capitalist and the high-tech entrepreneur will prove an exceedingly fruitful union.

7. The Coming Burst of Productivity and the New Entrepreneurship

The United States will have to deal with the twin problems of unemployment and inflation for the next three or four years. Our country has been experiencing a structural readjustment of its economy, and at the same time we have been fighting inflation, primarily by means of monetary policy.

The cost of money has been coming down, but unless the

federal government can reduce the large deficits looming ahead, the cost of money will be kept high enough to brake what otherwise would be rapid economic growth. Similarly, I believe it will be several years before we have adjusted to the transition from an industry-based society to an information-based society. Indeed, some aspects of this transition will last a decade and more.

Before explaining why I expect a new burst of productivity during the last half of this decade, I will put recent economic trends into context.

Between 1950 and 1970, the world experienced an era of rapid economic growth. The U.S. economy grew at a rate of 4.5% annually in real terms (i.e., discounting inflation). The Japanese and German economic miracles had growth rates twice as impressive. Resources were cheap, accessible, and easily exploited. Technology was the driving engine of our economy. It replaced labor, solved problems, and vastly improved our material well-being. This was a Golden Economic Era.

In the 1970s the climate suddenly changed. The price of energy skyrocketed, international business competition became murderous, the U.S. economic growth rate slowed to a crawl, and the outlook suddenly became bleak.

Given the relatively poor performance of the U.S. economy since the "oil shock" of 1973 and the "money shock" of 1981–82, why am I optimistic about a new burst of productivity? There are two compelling reasons. First, the wave of entrepreneurship I mentioned earlier—the 600,000 new companies being formed annually—will boost productivity. Most of these companies are based on the new technologies. Second, we are witnessing the creation of a new form of capital—venture or risk capital. In California, the number of venture capital investments has nearly doubled in the past two years. About $1 billion in venture capital—some would put the figure higher—are currently available for investment in Northern California alone. The size of investments is escalating rapidly, as well. A decade ago, $10 million was considered a large venture capital investment.

Recently a single deal was put together amounting to $150 million.

The reason this new development is important in the long run is that venture capital behaves differently from bank money. It is "patient" money, expecting a big payoff in the medium or long term. The venture capitalist typically uses a portfolio strategy—investing in a number of start-up companies at once, realizing that most will not succeed but hoping that one or two will pay out handsomely. An important side effect of this strategy is to shorten the time between the development of new technologies and their applications in the marketplace.

It is vital to understand why this is so. Traditionally, it has taken 20 years or more before a scientific discovery reached commercialization—transistors and computers are two classic examples. That interval is now shrinking. It is useful to think of this process as a horizontal line with science on the left-hand end, technology in the middle, and commercialization on the right-hand end. Science represents the discovery of a new principle (like the transistor or the semiconductor). Technology represents the promising applications of the technology (computers in the case of transistors, and microprocessors in the case of semiconductors). Commercialization represents the significant penetration of the marketplace by specific technological applications.

Science	Technology	Commercialization
(Discovery)	(Applications)	(Products)

/_____/_____/_____/_____/

      ideas to explore   prototypes

In the past, investment capital—banks—became interested only at the technology stage—that is, after the applications, and sometimes even the prototypes, had been developed.

Today, on the other hand, risk or venture capital is becoming interested in a discovery while its implications are still being explored—that is, before the applications are clear, let alone prototypes have been developed. Financial resources are being thrown into the development process far earlier.

Today many large corporations, having read the hand-writing on the wall, are beginning to function as venture capitalists themselves. Some have begun to acquire small, high-tech companies, which they then shelter and nourish under the corporate umbrella. Others have established internal corporate venturing programs, charged with taking technologies from their own laboratories to the market-place. Financial institutions, including pension funds, are beginning to invest a portion of their assets in high-tech companies. This availability of risk capital to the new wave of high-tech entrepreneurs is a profound change.

8. Government Policies and Corporate Responses

President Reagan has said he considers himself an "apostle of high-tech." In his budget proposals to Congress for 1984, he included large increases for support of basic research and science education, as well as for mission research (e.g., military research). Congress, too, has discovered high-tech. Congress today is in the mood to support the President on this issue and perhaps to "go him one better." Several hun-dred bills, proposed or on the docket, deal with science, technology, innovation, or education.

The U.S. government is rapidly developing policies to encourage technological development at all levels. The Administration's philosophy has been articulated by the President's Science Advisor, George Keyworth. The theme is that the government gets its greatest leverage through support of basic research. And, indeed, Washington is dra-matically increasing its support for basic research, while pulling back from support of applied research.

Today the separation of roles is clearer than in the past. The public sector now supports more basic research, while the private sector supports more applied research and development. The creative mechanisms that are being developed to facilitate close interaction between the two sectors I will examine below.

In 1980, in order to encourage commercial development of

new technologies, the government adopted a policy allowing universities and not-for-profit institutions (such as SRI) to retain ownership of inventions deriving from research funded by the government. Such research organizations could, for example, license their inventions (with some exceptions). This policy is intended to stimulate researchers to bring the fruits of their research to public use through commercialization.

These policies, along with tax policies favorable to research and development (R&D), industrial support for academic institutions, and more favorable depreciation schedules, have indeed stimulated private sector investment in science, technology, and commercialization. In 1981, for the first time in many decades, private sector support for R&D equalled public sector support—each spent about $34 billion. In 1983, we estimate that there was about $43 billion in support from the public sector and about $46 billion from the private sector.

The private sector has been responding to new opportunities in other ways as well. Most companies are actively searching for new products or improvements for old products. Most large high-tech companies such as IBM, GE, and AT&T used to take little positive interest in ideas developing outside their own laboratories. They rejected anything "not invented here." These companies have now changed their attitudes. They now ardently seek new ideas, whether originating inside their corporate laboratories or outside in universities, not-for-profit research institutes, and other commercial laboratories. Today their technology search is worldwide.

By and large, U.S. companies have grown bureaucratic and sluggish, but many large corporations are now looking for ways to encourage internal entrepreneurship. They are soliciting a more dynamic response from their managerial and technical staff. Some are actively attempting to change their corporate cultures to encourage employees to "own" their jobs—i.e., to be more creative and to take risks, to be more entrepreneurial.

Several significant technology-sharing efforts are under

way between competitors. The Electric Power Research Institute and the Gas Research Institute are examples of research institutions by means of which member companies in a common industry share research. Much of the research is placed in the public domain. The Semiconductor Research Institute is likewise supported by the semiconductor industry and shares research with its supporting members.

The new Microelectronics and Computer Technology Corporation (MCC) allows the 10 founding companies to support and engage in research in advanced computer technologies. The Justice Department is now taking a more liberal attitude toward technology-sharing agreements than in previous years. The sharing arrangements mentioned above have all received its approval.

9. The Crisis in U.S. Education

If the eight previous perspectives give us reason for optimism—and I believe they do—this last perspective poses a challenge as great as anything we have faced in recent history.

The educational system in the United States is not working well. If we do not make real progress rapidly on this problem (which is summed up very well in the Report of the Commission on Excellence in Education), we can forget all the grounds for optimism contained in the previous eight perspectives.

I think a great deal of progress is already being made on the educational front. Let me cite two examples from California.

The first is the new Center for Integrated Systems at Stanford University, sponsored by a number of U.S. companies. The Center's mission is to provide the United States with advanced high-technology graduates who can help the industry stay on the leading edge of computer-oriented technologies. Efforts like this are essential, in my view, if we are going to regain our leadership over the foreign competition.

A similar thrust is developing in secondary education in

California. I refer to the Institute for Computer Technology, which is sometimes called, erroneously, the "High-Tech High School." Actually, the Institute will have a broad-ranging curriculum stressing communication and classical disciplines as well as the new computer-oriented technologies. The project involves two school districts, Fremont and Los Gatos/Saratoga. It produces three types of high-technology graduates: the minimally skilled, such as assemblers; skilled technicians; and professional scientists/engineers. The last group are being prepared to go into institutions of higher learning, with the hope that they will then return to enter local industry in advanced high-technology roles. Industry wants people who are broadly educated as well as scientifically literate.

Classes at the Institute begin at 3:00 in the afternoon, when the conventional public schools close down for the day. Attendance is strictly voluntary; but students must perform satisfactorily to stay in the program, and the work load is quite demanding. Like the conventional public schools, the Institute receives funds, based on attendance,from the state education budget. Companies like Apple, Atari, and IBM have donated computers and other equipment, and IBM has seconded a senior executive for one year to help with the planning effort.

This new Institute planned its curriculum by seeking feedback from its beneficiaries. The high-technology companies that hope eventually to employ the Institute's graduating students contributed personnel to help with curriculum planning. While these industry people did not try to run the school or dominate the public sector participants, they did provide the essential inputs for this challenging project and are helping to train teachers in the new technologies.

The National Science Foundation and the Department of Energy have also taken up the challenge of enhancing science education at the primary and secondary school level. Funds have been provided in the President's Budget for 1984 to help develop science teaching, improve science curricula, and help train science teachers.

Virtually all the states are now undertaking major efforts to improve science teaching at the primary and secondary level.

In addition to the drive to enhance science teaching in formal programs, a large number of special summer programs such as the "computer camps" have been initiated to stimulate the interest of young people and to advance their training in specialized areas.

But promising as these new initiatives may be, they do not deal with the need to retool our adult work force. I am encouraged by the retraining programs set up for displaced workers by General Motors, the Autoworkers Union, and the State of California. This is a big step forward. I hope it will become a model for other states across the nation.

As a nation we are in transition. The problems are painfully obvious to all of us. But we have a great opportunity ahead of us. This nation has untapped human resources and an advantage in vitality compared to many other nations. If we can capture the energy of the new individualism, we will be headed for a new Golden Economic Era.

2. Challenges in Generating the Next Computer Generation

GORDON BELL

2. Challenges in Generating the Next Computer Generation

GORDON BELL

A leading designer of computer structures traces the evolution of past and present generations of computers and speculates about possible future courses of development for the next generations.

WHEN the Japanese told us about the Fifth Generation, we knew we were in a race. Ed Feigenbaum and Pamela McCorduck characterized it in their book, *The Fifth Generation*, but did not chart the racetrack. In the 1970s, while writing *Computer Structures* with Allen Newell, and recently in organizing the collection of The Computer Museum, I identified the pattern repeated by each generation. In order to win, or even to be in the race, knowing the course is essential.

The Cycle of Generations

A computer generation is produced when a specific cycle of events occurs. The cycle proceeds when

- motivation (e.g. the threat of industrial annihilation) frees resources;

- technology and science provide ideas for building new machines;
- organizations arise to build the new computing structures; and (after the fact)
- use of the resulting products confirm a generation's existence.

A generation results from at least two trips around this cycle, each succeeding trip an accelerated version of the previous one, as in a cyclotron. A newly perceived need (e.g. the "need" for personal computing) injects into this figurative accelerator the intention to "build a machine." New technology is then applied (e.g. in the case of the personal computer: the first microprocessors, higher-density memory and floppy disks), followed first by new contributions in system architecture and design, then by actual construction and manufacture. System software development further boosts the whirling "particle," and experimental use with relevant algorithms (e.g. Visicalc) completes its first cycle. Before it goes around again, critical evaluation is crucial. The particle is then accelerated again, until it attains the energy level necessary for use in practical applications and in industry.

In the past, two trips around this cycle tended to produce a generation of computers. The first trip generally resulted in a new structure, the second in a product with market acceptance. The personal computer (PC) followed something like this pattern, but required three cycles to reach the high energy level characteristic of a generation. The very first PC, the LINC, now in The Computer Museum, was built in 1962 and cost about $40K—the price of current engineering workstations. The PC concept was not viable from a market perspective until 1975, when the 4K memory chip and reasonably powerful microprocessors became available. The Apple II (circa 1978) using the 16K memory chip, and the IBM PC (circa 1981) using the 64K chip comprise the second and third trips around the accelerator.

Today one subgenerational cycle takes about 3 years to complete—the time it takes to develop a new technology—

with both industry and academe providing the push.

The Japanese Approach to the Next Generation

"If a computer understands English, it must be Japanese." (A pearl from Alan Perlis, speaking at The Computer Museum, September 1983)

The Japanese Fifth Generation plan, formulated in 1980, is based on worldwide research. Because the Japanese understand large-scale, long-term interactive processes, this research effort appears to be 3 to 5 years ahead of any such American effort.

The Japanese evolutionary approach to engineering and their leverage of the world's research have both been impressive. For example, they have chosen to develop a practical product from the concept of the Artificial Intelligence (AI) workstation—a concept long familiar in the lab and offered by Symbolics in 1980. They began with a Digital Equipment Corporation DECsystem 20 and are working to produce workstation hardware capable of executing Lisp and Prolog, 10 and 20 times faster than the DECsystem 20. In the process they hope to develop significant applications, which will allow them to use the workstation, evaluate it, and whirl around the cycle again at a higher performance level. Thus working with the natural pattern—starting with the criterion of usefulness, rather than devising arbitrary, revolutionary, and perhaps useless architectures—they envision completing two more cycles by 1990. Evolution has allowed them to gain supremacy in semiconductors and even supercomputers.

The United States Approach to the Next Generation

Because our efforts in the United States have until now involved a multiplicity of independent, uncoordinated inventions (many of them games), the Japanese may already have won the race to produce the next computer generation. As a guerilla army, so to speak, we have been drawn into the contest, lacking any notion of how this game should be played, with what combination of resources, and whether by fielding individuals or teams.

Consider, for example, the suggestions by MIT's Mike Dertouzos of ways we might still win in this competition with Japan:

1. Spend $100–200M to develop high-speed computers with AI functions.

2. Encourage increased openness toward foreign workers in U.S. industry and academia.

3. Provide tax credits for long-range investments that support a national technology policy.

4. Reexamine our antitrust policies with an eye toward permitting consortia in relevant industries.

5. Emphasize long-term research and development rather than our traditional short-term gains.

Each of Dertouzos's points raises questions:

1. Does the United States have a plan by which to coordinate the expenditure of several hundred million dollars? Our postwar university research has proceeded until now by means of small, decoupled projects. Can we quickly link such efforts up into large, interdependent, directed projects? Won't a larger budget simply raise salaries and swap a fixed set of people from place to place, because capital cannot be traded off instantaneously for labor?

2. Clearly we have been successful by free interchange of scientific knowledge. Would an open door policy toward foreign researchers and research results, although important for other reasons, necessarily increase our success in this immediate race?

3. Does the United States possess a long-range national computer technology policy that R&D tax credits might further? If not, tax credits could do little besides increase the earnings of the corporations enjoying them. Furthermore, regardless of tax considerations, few U.S. corporations are presently equipped to do research of the kind needed. Few U.S. corporate managers understand the differences

between advanced product development and mere product enhancement, let alone the best techniques in basic and applied research. While U.S. managers have trouble guiding the flow of ideas through the stages of product development within a single company, the Japanese have mastered techniques for transforming worldwide research into successful processes and products.

4. Are antitrust laws really a significant issue? The long gestation times of the several consortia that have been created in the United States were not due to obstructive FTC rules.

5. Are we prepared to abandon our usual emphasis on revolutionary machines in favor of a directed, evolutionary approach like that of the Japanese? The United States has tended to fund university projects based on the commitment of a single researcher or research group to a fascinating architecture. Such projects, which are really 10-year high-risk experiments not based on the need/use cycle, are especially vulnerable to loss of interest in midstream. We must learn from the Japanese how to define, establish, and execute projects in a way that does not violate the historically proven evolution.

The fate of the Fifth Generation is already cast. Can DARPA (Defense Advanced Research Projects Agency) provide leadership through the funding of univeristy research to enable the United States to reach the next generation successfully? In the past this agency has provided a "guerilla army" of researchers with funds to pursue timesharing, computerized speech understanding, graphics, packet switching, and, most recently, Very Large Scale Integration (VLSI). VLSI technology permits large primary memories, powerful microprocessors, Local Area Networking of personal computers, and architectures involving multiple processors to enhance performance and increase fault tolerance. DARPA's focus has always been on the funding of revolutionary new machines, some of which have aided progress toward new generations and some of which have not. Perhaps if we can clarify the successes and failures of the past we can draw useful conclusions about our potential for the future.

What Can Be Learned from Experimental Machines of the Past?

"[Building] experimental equipment merely for demonstration of [a] principle and without inherent possibility of transformation to designs of value to others does not [facilitate good] systems engineering." (Such was Jay Forrester's opinion when he headed MIT's Project Whirlwind, which produced an experimental computer that was eventually used as the prototype for the air defense system, SAGE.)

Table 1 displays information on the lifespans and usefulness of several university-based computers from the First to Fourth Generations. Development of the first four, from the Harvard Mark I/IBM ASCC to the Whirlwind, was driven by need: These machines saw use in the context of the critical manpower shortage following World War II. The Mark I, the first modern programmable machine, was put to work computing for the Navy immediately upon completion. Columbia's SSEC, derived from the Mark I, was a landmark in the history of computing because its development resulted in IBM's entry into computer building.

The University of Pennsylvania's ENIAC, built with backing from the Department of the Army, was the next revolutionary machine. By using electronic circuits instead of relays, ENIAC provided several orders of magnitude more performance than had Mark I or the Bell Labs relay-operated machines. The concept of the electronically stored program was original with ENIAC, which then led through the University of Pennsylvania EDVAC, Princeton's Institute for Advanced Studies IAS, and the University of Illinois ILLIAC I to the establishment of the computer industry.

Whirlwind, unlike the other machines listed, was built as a prototype for production. Its simple, straightforward, fast, 16-bit word, parallel design led directly to that of the SAGE computer. The SAGE real-time, interactive vacuum tube machines ran for 25 years without failure. Whirlwind's

Table 1 — Selected U.S. University-Based Computers

Machine	First Use	Concept-Use	Project-Use	Use	Use to Total Life	Results (in addition to engineer and scientist training)
Harvard Mark I — IBM ASCC	8/44	7	5	15	.7	Use, separate data and program memories
IBM SSEC	1/48	–	2.5	4.5	.6	Use, commitment to computers
ENIAC	6/46	4	3	9	.7	Use, stored program, Electronic Computer (program and data in one memory) design for EDVAC
MIT Whirlwind	6/50	5.5	3.5	9	.6	Use, circuits, core memory, real time and interactive computation, proto for SAGE system
ILLIAC I	9/52	4	3	10	.7	Use, proto for six others
MIT/Lincoln Lab TX-0	57	3	2	8	.8	Use, transistor circuits, large core memory
ILLIAC II	6/63	5.5	3	3	.3	Asynchronous logic, design too conservative
ILLIAC IV	11/75	12	8.5-10.5	6.5	.3	Use, parallelism (algorithms), accelerate bipolar memory development, stimulated competitive approaches
CMU C.mmp	5/75	5	4.5	6	.7	Parallelism, Intel 432 proto
CMU Cm*	9/76	4	2	>6	>.6	Parallelism, multibus-type structures
U. of Texas TRAC	83	7	5	>1	>.1	—

transistorized successor for the SAGE Project, the TX-0, took about a year to design and then remained in use for over 10 years. The Digital Equipment Corporation was based on the TX-0's well-enginered state-of-the-art circuits. The LINC computer, introduced in 1962, was so simply designed that in many cases it was assembled by its final users—the first build-your-own, interactive, personal computer with keyboard, CRT, and personal LINCtape filing system. It cost about $40,000, the price of modern workstations and could be easily moved from lab to lab. It was used by individuals running their own applications. And the MIT community during the 1950s and 1960s was a hotbed of users, who put together such machines to satisfy their desires to compute.

University of Illinois Computers

Ever since ILLIAC I, built on the IAS and von Neumann architecture, the University of Illinois has been a center for the building of new machines. Work at Illinois based on the circuitry and logic of the prototype IAS machine enabled such machines to be built at six other laboratories. The long-lived ILLIAC I's made significant contributions to our understanding of software and specific computer applications.

ILLIAC II, a transistor circuit based machine, went into operation three years after significantly better machines had become available (e.g. the IBM 1401 and 7090, the CDC 160/1604, and the DEC PDP-1). Its designers, aiming to produce a very-high-performance computer yet not faced with problems of mass production, selected conservative—even obsolete—technologies (e.g. germanium instead of silicon transistors, discrete wiring instead of printed circuits). The unwieldy result did not meet expectations. Consequently, the building of experimental machines at universities was squelched for some time.

ILLIAC IV developed from the Westinghouse Solomon

Project in 1962 but was not put into service until 1975.[1] A truly revolutionary machine, it operated at 250 million operations per second, its 64 parallel processing elements controlled by a single instruction stream. Its memory hierarchy for the processing elements—1 megabyte of RAM, 2 megabytes of core memory, and 139 megabytes of storage on a fixed-head disk—clearly violated "Amdahl's constant," which suggests 1 byte of memory is needed for each instruction per second executed.

Dan Slotnik, designer of the ILLIAC IV, recently commented to me:

> Most machines come about through evolution, and that's counter to the notion of original research which is supposedly the basis of university rewards. . . . I'm convinced that universities can't and shouldn't build machines. There are too many ideas, too much democracy, and too little discipline. I used to have to stop the flow of ideas on interconnection every week when we were designing ILLIAC IV. There is also too much bureaucracy. In a state university it takes 90 days to get an IC.

Larry Roberts, who headed DARPA while ILLIAC IV was being built, claimed the machine should have been executed with TTL (transistor-transistor logic) and not ECL (emitter coupled logic) technology. "People complain bitterly," he said, "but in the end conservative technology seems to work out better." The point is that a sacrifice of processing speed with the use of conservative technology— a sacrifice in instructions per second—may sometimes pay off in months of useful machine life if it gets the machine built significantly earlier than would be the case if more revolutionary technologies were used. Taking too long to get a machine operational limits its subsequent useful life and delays what is its essential purpose—i.e. to demonstrate whether its structure will advance computing.

Applied to certain problems, the ILLIAC IV was the world's fastest machine until the Cray 1 came into production. Its major contributions, however, were by-products: its design advanced our understanding of parallelism for single instruction, multiple data machines; it demonstrated

[1] R. Michael Hord, *The Illiac IV, The First Supercomputer.* Computer Science Press, Rockville, Md. 1981.

the use of fast semiconductor memories; and it stimulated commercial production of Texas Instruments ASC, Control Data Corporation's STAR, and the Cray 1.

Carnegie-Mellon University Multiprocessors

Carnegie-Mellon University's experimental machines, designed to obtain information about parallelism, were more evolutionary than the ILLIAC IV. The useful by-products of their construction also cost less than those of the University of Illinois machine by almost two orders of magnitude.

The idea that processors can be harnessed together in parallel to form powerful composite machines is intriguing because it means that high performance might be attainable not through massive designs but through repeated use of a relatively simple design. In the multiprocessor design, multiple instruction streams operate in parallel on multiple data streams. Multiprocessors were studied at Carnegie-Mellon in the late 1960s. Bill Strecker's 1970 thesis computed the performance for p processors accessing a common memory of m modules. This seminal work on multiprocessor structure was rejected for publication at the time because of relevance and originality; but during the last 10 years dozens of theses and papers have embellished Strecker's model, all referring to his early work.

The Japanese Fifth Generation Project is predicated on successful use of multiprocessor and dataflow parallelism. One researcher at the University of Illinois recently told me he wouldn't work on a multiprocessor project involving 32 processors unless it could be extended to 1000. Yet we have no evidence to date that more than a few processors can operate effectively in parallel on a single problem! Current research focused on exotic switching structures among thousands of processors and memories distracts scientists from the more difficult job of building even a small version of such a machine, and from what may be the impossible task of using one. Using a combination of new architecture, system software, language, and algorithm design, someone must first demonstrate that we can build a useful production machine involving 10 processors, before we extend this to a large-scale multiprocessor involving 100 or 1000 units.

C.ai and C.mmp In May of 1971 a multiprocessor comprising 16 processors was proposed as the first of the Carnegie-Mellon machines. The C.ai would have had one gigabyte of very high bandwidth memory and was intended for use in artificial intelligence research.

A much simpler design than this, using 16 Digital Equipment Corporation PDP-11 processor modules, was in design by August of the same year. Called C.mmp, this machine was used to examine the feasibility of multiprocessing and to develop a new "capability-based" operating system using a modification of the PDP-11. What was learned from the project is well documented in Professor W. A. Wulf's book, *Hydra*. The inability of this design to address all the memory available to it limited its usefulness. Furthermore, it was difficult actually to attain the maximum processing speeds theoretically possible. In order to be attactive to users a machine must offer more computational power than is easily available from other designs. By 1978 the Carnegie-Mellon University computing environment included other designs that were larger and easier to use than the C.mmp, which consequently was not used in production applications.

This project spawned the group that went on to design the Intel 432 processor. Clearly not everyone involved with C.mmp learned the lesson in limited memory addressing inherent in using the PDP-11 because the 432, too, suffered from the small address and excessive overhead that came out of the operating system approach.

Cm* An evolutionary descendant of C.mmp, Cm* is a set of computer modules that permits construction of a medium-scale multiprocessor (50 processors) in a two-level hierarchy, making the construction of a multiprocessor of over a 100 processors possible. Cm* uses concepts from C.mmp's operating system. From the point of view of any one processor, memory is conceived as three-fold: memory local to that processor; memory "pooled" by the cluster of 10 processors to which that processor belongs; and memory in another cluster. Any component processor in the multi-processor computer can access any memory available to the system, but each is designed to "prefer" local to cluster memory and intra-cluster to inter-cluster memory. The Cm* is thus problem-idiosyncratic, all access times varying with whether data are in local, in the cluster, or in another cluster's memory. Cm* is thus enabling researchers to study the relationships between hardware and software structures in parallel processing. Although significant work remains before the individual processors can work harmoniously together without extensive hand tuning of programs to suit particular interactions, the evolution of Cm* from C.mmp has already paid off. Now, a machine is needed that combines all the lessons learned in C.mmp and Cm*.

The Role of Future Research at Universities

Given our need for university research in the drive toward the next computer generation, what form shall the contribution of the universities take? Shall the research be done (a) by graduate students, (b) by nonacademic professionals within the university, or (c) by joint ventures between universities and outside companies? If the latter, shall funding come from the world of venture capital or from DARPA?

(a) Graduate students provide cheap, brilliant, but unpredictable labor. Reliance on students is not to be recommended unless the machine involved can be assembled easily from well-defined industry-standard modules. A major university infrastructure will be required if experimental machines are to be designed and hardware for them is to be fabricated within our universities.

(b) The presence of nonacademic computer professionals creates a second culture inside the university. Such a twin-cultured structure, being unstable, is somewhat difficult to manage, but it is essential to building a machine within the university. Carnegie-Mellon University was successful with this approach. MIT, too, established laboratories combining academic and nonacademic professional staffs, which produced such successful systems as Whirlwind, TX-0, TX-2, LINC, and the Multics™ timesharing system.

(c) Joint projects between universities and companies from the private sector often result in a hardware/software split, the university doing software. Digital Equipment pioneered in this form of interaction during development of timesharing on the DECsystem 10/20. For example, MIT and Stanford developed initial editors (e.g. SOS), assemblers, debugging tools (DDT) and compilers (e.g. LISP, SAIL). The most advanced joint project of this kind today is that involving Carnegie-Mellon University and IBM, who are working together on the creation of an educational computing environment in an IBM-provided industrial setting located on the CMU campus. Japanese companies build machines for their universities, especially the University of Tokyo. This arrangement has been used in developing previous generations and seems viable still.

We also see consortia forming among companies and universities for funding semiconductor facilities and for writing VLSI design software.

A related approach would use people from both academe and established industries, drawn into companies outside the university. These, funded by venture capital, would produce low-tech, low-risk products that might then fund projects to advance the state of the art. Many believe that such start-up company entrepreneurism is the way to beat the Japanese because it generates highly focused energy (one high-tech company, for example, recently developed and produced a UNIX product based on the Motorola 68000 chip in a period of 9 months); but I wonder whether the Japanese will be much daunted by our production of 123 kinds of 68000-based workstations? On the other hand, this arrangement—e.g. in the case of Amdahl's Trilogy Corporation—has funded really creative and advanced technology that no large corporation could fund because of the great risk involved.

Funding of computer science by the military often acts simply to churn a limited supply of researchers, moving them from place to place and raising salaries. The projects involved are typically large, requiring professors to become good managers in a university environment designed to employ them as good teachers. After a few years of work as a major-project manager at the salary of a teacher and in an environment lacking adequate engineering resources a professor may become an easy target for industry recruitment. In this way industry scoops up kernals of the nation's "seed corn."

Recent DARPA-funded research has tended to produce an algorithm, a program, a chip, or a system, whose development yields enough basic knowledge and a product idea promising enough to support a start-up company. Clark's Geometry Engine, for example, forms the basis for Silicon Graphics; the Timing Verify of Widdoes and McWilliams provides the basis for Valid Logic; and the Stanford University Network workstation is the basis of SUN Microsystems.

It is finally possible for people in the computer sciences to progress rapidly through the cycle from freedom to fame and riches by identifying and solving a problem while working in a research setting and then establishing a company to exploit their discoveries by developing the products of the next computer generation. Contrary to intuition, however, I believe that a surge in research funding will only move researchers from place to place and perpetuate further the erroneous notion that more money can instantaneously buy better scientific ideas and increase the available talent.

Breakthrough into the Next Generation

Leading computer scientists have proclaimed that the next developmental cycle, the one that will produce the Next Generation, will be driven by the demand among nonprogrammers for natural language communications capabilities based on breakthroughs in artificial intelligence. Since few genuine AI applications (e.g. "expert systems") are even now in operation, however, this view seems to me to be historically improbable. Nevertheless, the popular (and funded) belief is that revolutionary structures, implemented with VLSI and ULSI technologies and predicated on a high degree of processing parallelism, will be the key to these applications.

Past results suggest that basing the future on parallelism is risky, especially before a model of use for such systems exists as a design target. The only demonstrable parallelism today outside of vector machines (e.g. Cray 1) involves multiprocessors, which seem to be looked upon with renewed optimism in every generation. In the mid-1960s with large computers and in the mid-1970s with minicomputers, I felt that designing for multiprocessors was the best way to provide more computational power. Now, in the mid-1980s with their separate units becoming ever smaller, faster, and more powerful, use of multiprocessors must be an important way to increase performance—a fact reflected in the marketing of multiprocessors in all product ranges: supercomputers (Cray X-MP, Dennelcor), superminicomputers (ELEXSI), and microcomputers (Synapse).

With the advent of several commercial examples, it has become crucial for our universities to become involved in the use and further understanding of multiprocessors.

Why have multiprocessors not been used appreciably before now? It may be that in previous generations we have always found simpler ways, using technology or instruction set (e.g. vectors) to increase performance. Engineering may until now have been too conservative. Certainly operating systems and programming languages have failed to support or encourage multiprocessor designs. And conversely, there may have been no market for such machines because users have not been prepared to program them without language and operating support.

Human organization theory—the science of how human "processors" function (or malfunction) together—doesn't seem to contribute much to our understanding of parallelism, except anecdotally. More than a decade ago, for example, Melvin Conway speculated that people fashion computer structures to resemble the human organizations they know best. This may suggest why n individuals build n-pass compilers; why IBM builds hierarchically structured protocols like their System Network Architecture; why

DARPA maintains a store-and-forward net to have isolation between network and host computers; and why Digital builds democratic (anarchic) structures like Unibus, Ethernet, DECnet, and multiprocessors that can be employed very flexibly. Beyond such interesting notions, however, we lack an organization theory that can shed light on why it is as difficult to get more than six computer processors working together as it is to harmonize the work of six human beings, unless either group is wholly "top down directed" and given clear goals. Research should therefore concentrate for the moment on the general case of multiprocessors, because it has the greatest connectivity via primary memory. Slow or restricted networks such as Local Area Networks, trees, grids, hypercubes, etc., can be considered later, once we have understood the general case and the communications techniques it involves.

A glance at computer history reveals this pattern: New technologies lead to new computer structures (e.g. minicomputers, personal computers), which in turn create new companies. But only IBM and the large Japanese companies have so far demonstrated the basic understanding, the long-term commitment, and the marketing capabilities necessary to make the transition from one generation to the next. In both instances, however, someone else has had to establish the paths.

Where will the pathfinders arise today?

3. The Electronic University©

ROBERT SPINRAD

3. The Electronic University©

ROBERT SPINRAD

How will university life change in our computerized future? What human traits will resist the pressures of automation? Dr. Spinrad presents his view of things to come in the form of three episodes in the lives of the Student, the Professor, and the Administrator.

IN 1967 JOHN PIERCE, then of Bell Telephone Laboratories, in introducing a report to the President's Science Advisor observed that, "After growing wildly for years, the field of computing. . .appears to be reaching its infancy." Remarkably, a decade and a half later, the same thing can still be said.

This should not surprise us because, by its very nature, this incredible technology is open-ended, having no natural or logical limits to its utility. Programs build upon programs in a pyramid of value, each new layer providing increasingly rich tools and services. Some have likened the introduction of computers to the introduction of movable type in its effect on the social body. I find myself comfortable with that analogy, and am not at all reluctant to predict substantive changes to the essential workings of a university impacted by computers.

43

But my crystal ball is, alas, cloudy as to the *exact* shape of things to come. I have decided, therefore, to present my vision to you in the form of three vignettes: The Student, The Professor and The Administrator. These scenes are set in the very near future.

The Student

Rod walked into his dorm room, threw his book bag on the floor, flopped down at his desk and checked his mail.

Junk, junk, junk. The usual collection of announcements, trivia, on-line arguments and general trash. He disposed of them quickly.

But about a dozen items down the displayed list something caught his eye. The Swingtime Jazz combo was doing a gig that night at the Lion's Den, 9 o'clock. He'd be able to go. Great!

Humming to himself he flipped through the rest of the messages. A note from Paul about a borrowed disk. A Spring Fling had been scheduled. OK. He'd think about that—maybe Sara. A Humanities outing to the Met. OK. Junk, junk. He flicked the pointer down the screen. And then, wouldn't you know it, the very last message was labeled "Warning."

He read it quickly. It was from a guy in his AA 107 class, addressed to the whole class. He didn't know this Fred very well—chatted with him a few times at class breaks. Anyway, here was Fred, in a friendly note, saying that old Henderson had pulled a fast one on them. The assignment, instead of being the usual no-brainer, was very, very heavy. Fred wanted to alert everyone to that just in case they were thinking of leaving it to the last minute, which was just what Rod was planning on doing. Damn, damn, damn.

He pulled the assignment up on the screen. It looked innocent enough. "Read the first three sections of chapter 4." He glanced at his desk; yes, the book was there. "Read Henderson's Class Support Notes (5)." ("Class Support Notes"—that was a laugh. Old Henderson was just practicing on the class for his new book.) "Write a comparison of

Nozick's proposition with Taber's." Oh boy. There it was. Rod saw the jazz concert fade away.

He pulled the Class Support Notes up on the screen and started to read through them. It was a long text; a paper copy would be better. He punched the "hard copy" button and walked down the hall. By the time he got there the printer had produced the last page. Seventeen pages—damn! Rod riffled through the notes; there were diagrams, too! He reflected on what to do next, and quickly decided he'd go to dinner. On the way back from the service cluster he passed his room and threw the notes on his bed.

Thursday night was steak. At least that was good. On the way down he met Art and told him about Henderson's assignment and how it was going to screw up his evening. Art gave him one of those supercilious upper-classman smiles and asked him whether he had forgotten about the Student-Lib file system, an outgrowth of the old Fraternity File system. He had, in fact. He typically didn't use those files because there were sloppily organized and maintained. But this was different, and Art was right; that was the place to try. Rod bolted his dinner (even though he liked steak) and quickly returned to his room.

Student-Lib files were peculiar things. They contained old course material, class notes, random copies of old exams, student term papers, odds and ends. There was no money to maintain them—no Information Coordinator to keep them in shape—so they were structured only by the automatic data management programs the university kept around as utilities. Certainly a far cry from the professionally managed data and document bases that students and staff were used to. Nevertheless, there were times when they could be useful, and this was one of them.

Rod browsed through the file, cursing the weak, machine-generated cross-referencing schemes. It took him easily three or four times as long as usual to zero in on what he wanted, but find it he did! Three years ago Henderson had given a somewhat similar assignment. Fortunately, two students (probably nerds) had filed their essays. The automatic programs had picked up some of the keywords and so Rod was able to find the reports.

He read their analyses on the screen (they were short enough that it didn't pay to make a hard copy). Then, alerted to the important points, he read the chapter sections and the Support Notes.

It was 6:45, and the concert was at 9:00.

Was this "cheating"? Rod didn't know. But if it was, it was certainly part of an old tradition. And anyway, hadn't he heard once that it didn't matter how you got the ideas in your head, as long as you got them there?

Rod started typing. He had been using keyboards since he was a child and his fingers flew over the keys. He'd heard that, in the old days, veteran reporters prided themselves on being able to type faster than they could write. Of course; it seemed funny now that it had ever been a question.

About halfway through he stumbled. What was that Rawson demographics model? (He thought that it would look good to refer to it, and, feeling slightly guilty about this tawdry motivation, he decided to really learn something about it.)

He put the half-finished report aside (placing a tiny pointer to it at the corner of the screen) and called up the Rawson model. Now there was a retrieval system! Just a few keystrokes and the model with necessary tutorial text was on his screen. Where did it come from? Was it in the University library files or did the system have to reach farther for it? Rod wondered about that for a few seconds and then decided that it didn't really matter.

He worked with it for a little while, got the idea, and then applied it to his own data. He had spent more time than he thought he would, but it was actually fun. (He'd have to look up some more about this fellow Rawson.)

7:45. He thought he'd make the concert.

Back to the paper. Dismiss the Rawson model. Pull back the half-completed text.

He began going a little slower, thinking more about what he was saying and, for that matter, what old Henderson was really after. He actually looked up a few things he didn't absolutely have to. (It was easy enough, he rationalized; a few keystrokes and he had it.)

But then, sensing that he was reaching the end, he swung into full student-glib mode. Rolling phrases, extravagant similes and then—a full four minutes on the last sentence— he was almost through. But not quite. It would hardly pay to submit a slightly illiterate text, so he passed his paper through the service the students called RUF—the writer's friend.

RUF—with the artificial friendliness and somewhat cloying deference of a "human interface system"—pointed out "some possible spelling errors" and a few syntactical "abnormalities." It highlighted three places in the text where Rod might want to check his grammar. Of course, RUF was right. Rod made the suggested changes and a few others. And he was done.

He filed it (properly dated and identified) and sent a copy to the Henderson class submission file. He made a hard copy for himself just so he could carry it around. He felt good about it.

8:30. Plenty of time. He checked his mail again. This time he found a message from Laura. It seemed like a kind of personal thing to put on the electronic mail system. He read it through a second time and erased it.

Was there an admission fee for the concert? He called the announcement back up on the screen and was pleased to see that it was free. Out the door, Rod.

The concert was great! Even though it had been set up at the last minute, the electronic word had traveled fast and there was a big crowd. After a couple of encores the crowd spilled out into the quad a little after 11:00.

At 11:45 Rod checked his mail for the third time that night. He was tired but what he read really aggravated him. Some clown was claiming—and to a broad distribution list—that the University should stop subsidizing the Sunday band concerts in the quad. What an idiot! Didn't the guy understand anything about social values? He quickly typed a somewhat inflamed reply to the same broad audience—and sent copies to the band members.

"Let's see what they say about that," he thought as he fell onto his bed.

The Professor

Henderson arrived at his office shortly before 1 o'clock after the usual round of Saturday morning errands. Walking across campus from the burger joint he thought again about Ryad's article, the one he'd read last night. There was something disturbingly important lurking in that bland scholarly text, with all its footnotes and expansive explanations. It would be all too easy for someone to skim it and toss is aside, missing some of the quietly revolutionary things she'd said. (He smiled at the intellectual baby fat of this young postdoc. It just takes time to have enough confidence in yourself to be able to write directly and to the point without all the scholarly trappings.) Well, he'd help.

Sitting down at his screen he quickly typed a brief message calling particular attention to the article and dispatched it to the group of his colleagues most interested in this area—about 70 people at various institutions around the world. It was simple: in the "To" spot of his electronic mail form, he just typed "Positionist Group" and the system took care of the rest, looking up the names of the group members, determining how to reach them, and transmitting the text.

In the old days such a thing just wouldn't happen. One could hardly imagine coming into one's office in the morning and making 70 phone calls to colleagues suggesting that an article might be worth reading. Or writing 70 letters. Or writing one letter and sending out 70 copies. No. The effort involved would clearly signal the action as suspect, or at least odd. But, with the electronic mail system as effective as it now was, such a friendly note was quite routine—normal and collegial—just because it was so easy and straightforward.

But he hadn't come in to do that. The only reason he and his wife had put off driving to the cabin until tomorrow was that he had to catch up on some things and, most importantly, prepare all of next week's lectures. He was going to be so tied up that this was the only day he had. (Of course he could have handled it all from his home workstation, but he'd really wanted to get out of the house. Hadn't exactly told Jane that.)

Fortunately, Henderson had taught this course many times before so it wasn't as if he had to start from scratch. He pulled up his lecture notes from the last time he'd given the course, two years ago.

Well, maybe he was getting lazy, as Jane said, but it looked as if, for the most part, they'd do. They needed some updating, and he'd do a better job on the new material, he rationalized, because he could build on the base already established.

Current. Relevant. Topical. That's what he was after. He wove some recent news clips into the illustrative material, picking some particularly striking color shots. The TUTOR program, an old standby of his, made it easy to structure and display the lectures. With only a modest amount of advance notice to the library, he could present an astonishingly diverse array of materials on the classroom screen—pictures, charts, models, even animation (although Henderson didn't use this much). The lecture outline, of course, only appeared on the screen at the podium.

Just as he was starting on the outline for the Friday lecture he was startled by the phone's ring. It was Dean Croft. Henderson started to mention his surprise that the Dean was there on Saturday but then thought better of it. (Deans, too, have a lot of work to do, apparently.)

There had been a complaint from a parent and Croft had been given an earful that morning. While the Dean was talking, Henderson swiveled in his chair and brought the student's file up on the screen—a kid named Rod Jackson. An erratic record. Periods of excellent performance interspersed with lackluster ones. Something was wrong. He was embarrassed that he hadn't noticed it himself. He stared at Rod's picture but was troubled to find that he couldn't place him clearly in the freshman class he taught.

Henderson and Croft had a long and somewhat inconclusive conversation. The professor agreed to speak to the young man and, when Croft hung up, he sent Rod a message asking him to drop by his office. Henderson stirred up a cup of coffee and wondered whether the University, with all its wondrous communications modes, wasn't neglecting the most essential one!

Well, back to work. He did a more thorough revision of Friday's lecture, allowing a greater amount of time for discussion (was that a coincidence?) and for a brief profiling of the people involved.

Completing his preparations, Henderson notified the library's Resource Scheduler to expect heavy student demand for a file he knew to be located across the country. (The scheduling algorithm would decide whether to establish a local copy for the high-use period.)

He pulled up the homework assignment forms, filled them out and dispatched the message to the class, along with a personal note. (The earlier conversation still preyed on him.) Edgy, he decided to go out for a walk.

One turn around the campus and he returned to his office refreshed.

There was this idea for a paper he'd had—just notions flitting about in the back of his mind. He'd been looking forward to browsing through the literature in the field. Start with a key contributor—Junko. Henderson typed in the name and was rewarded with a list of Junko's articles for the last four years.

Selecting one, he called it to the screen and started reading. No. Not the area he was thinking about. Try another. Yes, closer. This was interesting and promising. He didn't bother following up on the first and second references but the third seemed, for his purposes, to be more important. He pointed to it on the screen and the article, after a short delay, appeared. (Where had it come from? He guessed only the librarians could track that one. No matter.)

The new article led to another one which, in turn, led to a third. Thoroughly engrossed, Henderson didn't notice the passage of time.

The third article talked about a "Hammersmith Community." What was that? No references were provided. Henderson highlighted the term and asked for a search. The
pause was a bit longer this time, but a list came back. He
dug in, burrowed around and, to his surprise, came out in
somewhat unfamiliar terrain. So he reversed the direction
of his intellectual zoom lens and asked for a broader, rather
than a narrower, context. Again, the system obliged,
although not as helpfully. (Specific to general is harder to
program, his computer science friends told him—at least so
far.) It took a lot more browsing before he was comfortable
with the material he was getting. (Fortunately, the system
was keeping a road map of his search. That way later, if he
wanted, he could reconstruct the thread through the
diverse articles in the various journals that all played on the
Hammersmith theme.) Finally, he tried a few "fuzzy
searches," but the sweep was too broad and he couldn't
cope with the torrent of only slightly relevant information.

Enough for now—and quite a bit to think about. He was
hungry and late. He called his wife, made apologies (she
was resigned) and went out for a snack. (She agreed to
make other plans.)

On his return he checked his mail. Nothing special since
yesterday. One message was from a colleague in Taiwan
(apparently sent on Sunday, which was tomorrow). The
fellow was seeking some specific information about the
recent United States/Japan codicil. Henderson pulled up
the Department copy on his screen. It was heavily marked
up (in an electronic sense). Some notes were his; others
were pointers to comments by other people. There were
even two voice annotations (shown by the little image of the
telephone next to the paragraph). He touched one and
smiled at the gruff, curmudgeonly voice; no one could ever
mistake Watson. (For him you really didn't need the screen's
name identification.) Yes, yes. Watson's view was clear and
forceful, but no one in the Department would be particularly surprised at what he had to say. But no, nothing bore
on the specific question.

Henderson thought it inappropriate to share any of his

colleagues' off the cuff comments with the Taiwan university so he cleared the screen copy of all its annotations, typed a cover message attaching the codicil and, apologizing for not having an answer to the question, sent it off.

He sent a copy of the original query to Torrey, the Department's Information Coordinator, asking whether he could help. He was careful not to send a copy of the second message to the Taiwanese because he didn't want to appear to be committing Torrey, who was always complaining about overload. You had to be careful about these things.

Now, one last task before he called it quits. The book he was editing was in its final stages. Hayes (always the last one) had finally transmitted his chapter, and the other authors were bleating about the delay.

He displayed the text in composition mode and began editing. He was mainly concerned with the material's appearance since the content had already been painstakingly reviewed. This was pleasing work. Henderson felt that he could understand the pride that printers took in the production of a truly handsome book.

Today, the screen obeyed the what-you-see-is-what-you-get rule, so he could savor the exact appearance of the final printed page, with the varieties of typefaces, sizes, and emphases accurately displayed. Further, the screen image faithfully duplicated the graphs, charts, diagrams, and pictures in their proper positions.

Editing, then, consisted of moving things around on the "page," changing sizes and positions until the image was attractive. The process was fun.

The advantage, of course, was that the electronic file behind the screen image was the master from which the book would be typeset. This eliminated typesetter's errors, saved considerable time, and was viewed by Henderson and all his colleagues as a great improvement over the way things used to be.

He stored the book file, awaiting only the *Acknowledgments* page, before he did the final touch-up and first run of copies.

It was 10:00 p.m. and, as Jane would impatiently say, he'd

"spent another day at his damn screen." But there were a few things to clean up.

He triggered the calendar program to try to find a meeting time for the curriculum committee. He sent a voice message to his mother. He read the minutes of the last meeting of the Faculty Senate.

Then, just for fun, he retrieved the University's electronic bulletin board. Ads. Rides to share. Protests. Causes. Jokes. Urgent pleas. Concert announcements. (He'd missed a good one last Thursday.) In a funny way you could take the pulse of the University by reading the bulletin board. Up. Down. Tense. Easy. The beat of the community flowed before your eyes on this glowing screen.

Funny! Henderson thought about the built-in contradictions as he closed the door of his office.

The Administrator

Dean Croft got in early after her run. There were mornings—and this was one—when she thought the answer to her overload problems was to beat the staff to the office and get a quiet headstart on the day. She checked her calendar. The blinking entries reminded her of things she had to do that day. (Some were "tickler" entries that either she or Dick, her assistant, had previously put in; others were automatically generated by the administrative calendar system.) Nothing out of the ordinary. Only two really time-urgent ones.

The first, sending out the research proposal to the Council on the Arts, she handled herself. The budget office had completed and filed the financial forms and tacked on the administrative boilerplate. She typed a cover message to the whole package (sufficiently gracious she hoped) and sent it off.

The second was a little touchier. The C-School Visiting Committee was starting its two-day session with a dinner that evening. She was scheduled to give the welcome and charge-to-the-committee talk, but Wriston still hadn't told her the outcome of that hot curriculum argument. She sent a note to Wriston, and a copy to her assistant, saying she had to talk to him before 5 o'clock. Dick, seeing the message when he came in, would know enough to follow up— vigorously!

She took a quick look at the *New York Electronic Times* headlines and then went on to her mail. Oh, look at all that stuff. She'd unloaded the mail file last night before she left the office, but look at all the messages that had come in since! Some had been sent yesterday and had come in overnight, primarily from schools to the west. But the bulk of it was from local faculty and staff. (At times like this she considered the home workstations to be a mixed blessing. For a moment she regretted not having set the automatic mail sorter to send a polite response to some of her correspondents saying that the Dean "was away until Friday but would certainly reply as soon as possible." But she quickly squelched the thought. It was the responsibility of Deans (she mentally sighed) not be be "away until Friday."

She scanned the list of senders quickly and chose to read—out of sequence—one from Sovenhower, the President. It seemed that the President, at the Trustees' dinner last night, had been asked to give a talk, two weeks hence, on "the role of the university as a catalyst for social change." Before he retired for the night and because he knew that "time was short," Sovenhower had sent Croft a message asking her to "work up some ideas." Surprise—and extra work—was, it seemed, an ever-present element of this job.

Croft decided on a two-pronged assault. First she sent a note, with the President's message attached, to her assistant and asked him to browse electronically through the Sociology Library database for relevant material. Dick was a well-organized chap and liked to operate the search programs; he called it "prowling the world's information thicket." And of course his "prowls" were aided by the multiple paths blazed—and the threaded trails left behind—by scores of previous scholars.

Next, she sent the message off to Torrey, the Information Coordinator. (No matter how smart those computer science folks were, they'd never produce a program that would replace the human mind for sorting, sifting, and recalling ill-defined or poorly characterized snippets of information. Or at least Croft hoped that was so.) Torrey, she felt, would give the request more than casual attention when he saw its source.

The two probes launched, Croft entered a "tickler" into her calendar system and went out into the hall for the regular morning coffee-and-danish break.

She and Lee chatted about a facilities problem until her 10:30 budget meeting. It was just a week before the scheduled submission and a large group had assembled. Buchanan, the chief budget officer, summarized. This was the first year in the last three that there had not been some sort of financial crisis. She put the source and application of funds tables up on screen and touched on the key issues for each of the major entries. There were a lot of "what if" questions which she quickly explored on the displayed financial spreadsheets. Croft was old enough to remember when these kinds of manipulations took days—or weren't done at all because of their difficulty. How quickly new things became useful—and then necessary. Why, she could remember when students had had to stand on long lines to register for classes. How odd, to think of it now.

In those days, when computers were new to the university, the debate had raged about how to charge for them. Computer time and services were expensive. You couldn't just *give* them away, could you? So a variety of schemes had been developed to ensure that these valuable assets were properly paid for and efficiently utilized around the clock. Students, for example, were charged less and had more responsive services if they did their computer work from ten p.m. to six a.m. That made sense, didn't it? Faculty, for their part, battled over scarce research computer time.

Then, one day, some wag had written a piece for the student newspaper suggesting how to cut costs and make more efficient use of books at the library. The plan was simple: the University would time-share books, with readers taking turns throughout the day. The less privileged readers would, of course, be scheduled for the midnight-to-dawn shift but would be charged less.

The parody had had an electrifying effect. All of a sudden everyone understood! Computers and databases were to the twentieth century university what books had been to the sixteenth century one! Basically, people had to change the way they looked at things.

But the ensuing political battles had been fierce. They were only really settled when a wise university president declared the libraries to be the winners—but quickly added that all major new library expenditures would be for computing, database, and communications equipment. Since then, as is well known, the libraries had become heavily electronic.

It was funny, but a lot of the changes now taken for granted had been forced on the university by the students. Not in a '60s-type revolution but by an '80s-type one. In the '80s, freshmen had begun pouring into the universities with personal computers packed in with their jeans and stereo equipment. After putting up their posters, filling their drawers, and setting up their speakers they had looked around their dorm rooms for the computer jacks. But except in some pioneering schools, the information jacks hadn't existed.

For the fact was that these students, these children of the information age, were ahead of their elders in understanding the nature of the revolution that was taking place—the information revolution. And it was their impatience that—in no small part—pressed these new structures onto the somewhat stodgy university body.

It had been somewhat rocky at first, Croft remembered, but the young people were right. A colleague of hers once said that students were the "crabgrass in the Grove of Academe." But Croft knew better and she suspected that her colleague did also. Universities had to lead and, Croft ruefully acknowledged, more often than not the impetus came from the younger members of the traditional "community of scholars."

She was still thinking about change as she strolled toward the Faculty Club for lunch. Henderson had been talking about some ideas he'd been playing with. They looked very promising and, with these new systems, you could chase things down so much faster than you could in her day. She'd actually, at odd moments, been learning how to run the new browsing searches. Dick, ever the enthusiast, had been eager to help, and was clearly pleased that his boss was so interested.

As she walked through the door she resolved to block out some time that afternoon to do a little browsing and thinking. Maybe, she thought, there were still a few years of good scholarship left in her old bones.

Epilogue

I hope, through these somewhat fanciful vignettes, to have given you a sense of what the future university might be like. But I must confess that writing them did not particularly stress my abilities as a seer since so many of the things I've talked about today already exist in one form or another. I have simply tried to weave separate threads into a pattern that could seem reasonable to you.

What literary qualities these scenes may lack will, I hope, be compensated for by the intensity of my conviction that these remarkable technologies will have a profound effect on all the ways of our lives. And that those who work with words and ideas will be the most affected.

I was first introduced to computers at this great university some 30 years ago. And I must tell you that I find myself as fascinated and excited by them today as I was on that very first magical day.

4. Modern Computing: A Force for Diversity or Conformity?

EDWARD E. DAVID, JR.

4. Modern Computing: A Force for Diversity or Conformity?

EDWARD E. DAVID, JR.

The power of modern computing has led on the one hand to conformity and centralization, and on the other to greater diversity and decentralization. An analysis of society's options in the dawning information age leads to Dr. David's emphasis on the importance of educational, cultural, and political values in charting the way between unhappy extremes.

IBM IS USING the image of Charlie Chaplin's "little tramp" to promote its personal computer. Most experts consider it a brilliantly successful advertising campaign, and IBM's success dramatizes a fascinating shift in popular attitudes. Recall Chaplin's famous role in the film "Modern Times." There Chaplin portrays a worker dehumanized by the demands of the technology of the production line. At quitting time he cannot stop repeating the monotonous motions involved in putting the same nut on the same bolt of the same unidentified machine throughout the workday, and he can't escape the boss's gaze even in the bathroom. Now IBM portrays computing technology as a way out of the dehumanizing conformity imposed by older technologies. And, clearly, the public buys the idea.

The recent film "War Games" goes even further,

suggesting that the personal computer is a powerful tool for asserting individuality against the conformity demanded by centralized systems. A drawback is that in the process of this assertion the young hero almost starts World War III. Then, after the release of the film, in one of those developments that thrill every promoter, the nation saw life imitate fiction in the high jinks of Milwaukee's "414" boys. Naming themselves after their city's area code, these young men used their home computers to make mischief in mainframes all over the country, including an unclassified system at the Los Alamos Laboratories. So, as the year of Orwell's novel, *1984*, approaches, we are finding that we should be worrying not only about "Big Brother" but about "Little Brothers and Sisters" as well!

In both good and bad, culture follows technology. People would not have come to live in "vertical cities" like New York without the development, first, of structural steel and elevators. Similarly, we have seen what installation of fixed-rail systems, such as subways, can do to urban form. Commercial businesses, condominiums and apartment houses, and enterprises of all sorts tend to cluster around the stations, raising property values and resulting in a corridor-like development form, with all that this implies for living conditions.

In computing, the technology for many years led toward increasing centralization and conformity, as organizations sought to take advantage of the economies of scale associated with large computers. Now, with the advent of higher levels of circuit integration and microcomputers, the trends are heading more strongly in the opposite direction—toward distributed computer processing, greater decentralization, and diversity. In the long run, will computing become a force for diversity or conformity? The importance of the question extends beyond Hollywood. For as computing and communications come together, they are becoming the dominant force of the dawning information age. So the question impinges on some of our society's most critical values and concerns.

We know that to a degree centralization and conformity

promote economic efficiencies, social cohesiveness, and national strength. On the other hand, we know that centralized systems must make room for individuality and diversity if they are to promote human creativity, technological innovation, entrepreneurship, and economic growth. Indeed, the recent bestseller, *In Search of Excellence,* shows in convincing terms how important "loose structures" are to keeping business organizations innovative and vital. Great business organizations are thoroughly premeated by a strong sense of mission; yet some of their most useful innovations are "bootlegged" by product champions who work more or less outside the usual system for command and control. As a society, we value a sense of mission and ethical commitment. We value what these bootleggers do, too. And we value human freedom as almost an absolute.

Organization

Obviously, we seek an optimum combination of the diversity that new computing environments can provide and the conformity that is still required to maintain them. As a major user of computing technologies, my own organization, Exxon, has a strong interest in meeting the challenge successfully. Here I will explore briefly how that challenge is shaping up in three representative areas familiar to me. First I'll consider the role of modern computing technologies in advancing science and technology, with a look at what my own company is doing at our new research center in Clinton Township, New Jersey. Then, I'll turn to the issue as it affects the office, the factory, and the consumer.

Finally, I will close with a few thoughts about how computing trends are affecting the relationship between the individual citizen and government. In rather simplistic terms, the question here is whether computing technologies are encouraging tyranny, anarchy, or something in between. My answer favors the "in between," with a strong bias toward the advantages of diversity conferred by increasingly more powerful hardware-software systems. The actual outcome will of course depend upon prevailing social and political values: computers do not tyrannize people, people do. Nor can computers make the world fly apart into anarchy or worse, but people *can*. The effect computers will have will hinge upon education not only in computer science but also in the arts and humanities, for in those disciplines lies the essence of human values.

Research and Development

As a tool for advancing science and technology, the invention of computing is having the same revolutionary impact as the inventions of the telescope and microscope. As the noted science historian, Derek de Solla Price, has said, those instruments broke through the limits imposed by the *naked eye;* computing has broken through the limits imposed by the *naked brain.*

In research and development, as elsewhere, the central fact about computing today is of course that the cost curves have crossed: almost regardless of the measure used, computing is rapidly becoming cheaper relative to human labor. The era of free love in our society is being joined by the era of free logic and free memory. Under the pressure of these trends, computing has evolved from conformity toward diversity. The clear trend is toward extensive local, personal computing available from powerful desktop and laboratory computers at the researcher's fingertips.

At the same time, most organizations, including Exxon, are preserving enough conformity to allow for extensive networking and communications—that is, loose computing structures. No matter how powerful local processing becomes, scientists and engineers still need equipment for rapid sharing of information and ideas, and for sharing access to large data bases, high-quality printers and graphic output, and supercomputers.

The analogy to the automobile is often invoked. The auto has brought us extraordinary personal mobility and independence, but not without common roadways, common rules of the road, and common performance standards for exhaust emissions, mileage, and the like. Likewise, present computing trends offer greater scope for personal initiative and creativity, not only through personal control of computing resources but also through convenient interaction with other minds and with scientific and engineering reality. Highly important in this regard will be software systems that provide essential support to inexpert users. Many scientists and engineers are now using computers as easily as drivers use the automobile, without needing to know what's under the hood.

It is not obvious that decentralized, interactive computing really will boost productivity in science and engineering. I recall debates during the 1960s about whether interactive computing would enable programmers to create software more efficiently or merely encourage them to try more things without thinking deeply. The scientific side of this argument was that facile computing would discourage development of both theory and analysis. It is certainly true that in science, computing has made it easy to collect and manipulate massive amounts of data. For example, in modern spectroscopy, investigators can search many more parameters and obtain thousands of times more data points than they could in precomputing days. But some question whether we have seen a proportionate increase in the rate of scientific understanding. Regardless of that concern, the most profound effect of making computing widely available has been to increase the market beyond all expectations. If the majority rules on the scientific benefits of computing, the ayes clearly have it.

At Exxon Research and Engineering Company, we look forward to the benefits of "loose structures" in computing. The hub of our new computing systems will eventually be desktop workstations of extraordinary power. They will integrate in one system, engineering and scientific computing; office and administrative computing, including word processing; information management and retrieval; and text, data, graphics, and voice communications inside and outside the company. Industry is approaching but has not yet attained what we have in mind, so at our new research facility in Clinton Township, New Jersey, we have adopted an interim strategy that will allow us to incorporate the comprehensive workstation when it arrives. For now, we will rely on an advanced voice-data switching system manufactured by an Exxon-associated company called InteCom, Inc. to integrate a carefully planned mix of systems based on word processors, laboratory computers, and a timesharing computing system. The total will incorporate most of the features that a complete research facility requires.

Let me cite three research applications that typify how we are using computing. The first illustrates the ubiquity of "smart" instruments that incorporate computing systems for laboratory application. In one of our labs, a hierarchy of computers not only controls experimental conditions in two microreactors for testing catalysts but also suggests new experimental conditions, helping the scientist to chart an optimum course through the maze of data that the system could collect. A little further down the innovation chain, we have developed for the Clinton labs a multi-tiered, distributed system of micro- and minicomputers that operates and acquires data from some 24 pilot plants, as well as performing data management and analysis, raising the productivity of those plants manyfold.

My third example is more generic: computer modeling. Such models are a potential avenue for reducing the need for pilot plants, which in the petroleum and petrochemical industries often cost many millions, even hundreds of millions, of dollars. The example has bearing on the current debate about how to finance the development of the next generation of supercomputers. Modeling is often considered a centralized activity, since a realistic model of a coal liquefaction process, for example, demands a fast, powerful computer. Exxon has been doing mathematical modeling for years, and we do make extensive use of supercomputers in some areas—for example, seismic exploration. But, more importantly, in many other areas where Exxon is active, computing power is even today outrunning the fundamental science required for robust models. Before we can develop such models, we need far deeper understanding in such areas as chemical kinetics, turbulence, multiphase systems, and much more. Thus, in this cycle of the evolution of computing, the state of science itself now favors decentralized approaches in many disciplines, while perhaps whetting appetites for new rapid stepups in supercomputing at a later time.

In any case, it is safe to say that today's trends in computing strongly support the kinds of "loose structures" we identify as the most fruitful for research and development. As I've suggested, such trends do not optimize themselves. More than a little centralized decision-making is required— for example, to assure that there is compatibility between hardware and software, and to ensure that people, workstations, and computers can conveniently communicate and share central resources. But decentralized systems show the greatest promise for enhancing the ability of researchers not only to acquire data, but also to manipulate concepts, models, and symbols rapidly, helping them to fathom the meaning of the data. Some of our finest research people at Exxon Research and Engineering have learned to "think like a molecule"—showing keen intuition congruent with reality. Our goal is to help computing evolve in directions that will best serve such individual intuition. A word of warning was sounded here by Professor Robert Merton. He recalled Whitehead's fallacy of Misplaced Concreteness: the confusion of the model with reality. The originators of computer models usually won't make such mistakes, but users may.

Regardless of this crucial issue, success in fashioning a modern computing environment will depend not on computing but on those human values that have always distinguised great research centers—that is, on the one hand, a strongly shared respect for the individual contribution, leading to an awareness that research initiatives are best retained by the researchers themselves; and, on the other hand, a strongly shared sense of mission and objectives, and a habit of evaluating results with those missions in mind.

The Office, Factory, and the Marketplace

As computing increasingly enters the office, the factory, and the marketplace, the necessity for loose structures will become obvious there too. Thus, in the modern office there will be a certain de-skilling of jobs. With the help of a word processor, an average typist now can produce as accurate work as a keyboarding expert can. But using an advanced word processor or a desktop computer will require a level of personal knowledge and judgment that using a typewriter does not. Modern computing is not merely automating the old ways. Rather, it is creating new needs for flexible people to restructure the old ways. We will need fewer rote skills of the kind satirized by Chaplin in "Modern Times" and more personal initiative, systems thinking, and imaginative concern with the organization's objectives and how to achieve them.

The advent of the industrial robot has dramatized the impacts of modern computing technologies on industrial production. The petroleum industry was one of the first to show these impacts. As semiconductor and computing technology developed over the past 20 years, the petroleum refining and petrochemical industries found they could add progressively more complex control systems and control strategies to their plants. Exxon now has some 100 computer control systems installed in refineries and chemical plants around the world. Do the results tend toward diversity or conformity? Here, too, the tilt is toward more flexibility and diversity, but with due regard for product quality standards and the efficiencies that can be obtained through integrating the elements of large and complex plants.

In the manufacturing industries, the means for achieving higher quality, lower cost, and better designs include what are called flexible manufacturing systems. These systems integrate robots, intelligent machine cells, and computerized scheduling and inventory control. They should in time revolutionize the low- and medium-volume manufacturing that accounts for a large share of our gross national product—in fact, a share far greater than that of mass-produced items like automobiles. In theory, the components of the new manufacturing systems can be rapidly reprogrammed from making, say, lawn mowers today to making snow blowers tomorrow, thus preserving flexibility and holding down capital costs. I say "in theory" because not many manufacturers who bought such reprogrammable components off the shelf today would know how to create a system that would serve their needs effectively. This implies that industry will adopt the new systems in evolutionary rather than revolutionary fashion, allowing time for the workforce and the management to adapt.

We can see only dimly where all this is leading. Consumers are sure to benefit from some combination of lower costs, greater product diversity, and higher quality. Some workers will face fewer employment opportunities. But many others will find a diversity of new jobs that demand distinctly human qualities. It goes without saying that an important social responsibility in the coming years will be to ease the transition for people, perhaps chiefly through diversifying and improving access to our educational systems.

The Citizen and Government

But when the history of the information age is written, the historian will perhaps *not* assign primary importance to the impact of computing technologies on science and technology, the office, or manufacturing. Instead he may well assign it to the dramatic diversity of life styles that personal computing appears to be in the process of generating. We often hear about the possibilities of the electronic cottage, with people communicating to work, traveling only for pleasure. The networking capabilities of personal computers will surely multiply opportunities for work, entertainment, and shopping in the way that newspapers, radio, and TV have. New "asynchronous" communities are springing up, whose members communicate about their common interests without regard for the barriers of time and geography. To be sure, they are doing so with the benefit of considerable standardization in communications protocols, software, and hardware.

However, it is also possible that the future historian may emphasize a more ominous side of the information age— the way it has enhanced government or corporate power to enforce conformity. Today, such fears often focus on massive data banks collected by both private and government agencies. The data banks find applications ranging from nuisances like junk mail and zip code marketing, to serious law enforcement. In Massachusetts, officials have sought to halt abuse of the welfare system by cross-checking data on people collecting welfare with data on people holding state jobs. The U.S. Internal Revenue Service has announced a plan to match "life style" data compiled by various business information services with its own files in order to identify prime candidates for tax audits. University researchers familiar with the strings attached to federal research grants—such as the infamous circular A-21—need not be told about the extraordinary informational demands that government has imposed in the name of "accountability." In many cases it is prudent to assume that information supplied for one purpose may eventually be used for quite another. It is becoming more and more difficult to live anonymously in the interstices of society as many people prefer to do. And the underground economy is becoming more enticing, not only for tax advoidance, but also for simple privacy.

Still, remember that modern computing has enhanced the powers of Little Brother, too. It has multiplied the power to search the haystack, but it has also multiplied the straws in the haystack. Few people would deny government all resort to technologies, since some degree of conformity among Little Brothers is essential if the state is to meet legitimate social and legal responsibilities. And of course we already have many safeguards in our law that limit the way government and individuals can use information. We may need to extend these safeguards to enable individuals to ensure at the very least that information about them is accurate and to know exactly who has had access to and has used such information.

Better security systems will help. The events in "War Games" could never have occurred as described, because secured Defense Department networks are not accessible by outside telephone. Some other government and business systems can prevent all but the most determined and sophisticated users from breaking in. Nevertheless, these are less secure than our defense systems, and still others are entirely insecure because of the practical need to allow users easy access. Once someone does have access today, it is impossible in most cases to prevent him from getting at the files he wants. What is required here are systems, such as the Multics™ system marketed by Honeywell, that separate different classes of users. In future secure systems, we should be able to demonstrate mathematically that unauthorized users cannot break in within a specific timeframe. The currency of information is the well-known essence of practical security, since it is neither feasible nor necessary to keep all information secret forever. I have been speaking of the security of the technology itself. We will require other security techniques, and most of all human integrity, to ensure that individuals do not let slip what they know to the wrong people. Again, success here will hinge upon education combined with integrity, as contrasted to mere changes in laws and regulations.

But in my view the future historian will stress an even broader effect of the new computing technologies than the special uses and abuses of large data banks. Computing is creating great pressures to rationalize all our industrial, educational, and societal processes. In vast areas of our national life most decisions are still made according to rule-of-thumb, gut feeling, or dogma. Certain decisions cannot wait to be made in the light of information that could eventually or even immediately be found, or of analysis that could be performed on that information. But modern computing is paving the way for vastly more sophisticated decision systems. Will these decision systems be used to enforce uniformity or to preserve diversity? Can we preserve enough leeway in society to keep people from believing either that they are being singled out or that they are being completely ignored as individuals? With such systems, can we retain human values, including our political rights and freedoms? I am sure we can, but the feat will require education in the broad sense of the term, education not only in computer science but also in the humanities and arts where values are studied and expresssed.

Summary and Conclusion

Modern computing is a prime mover in the societywide "megatrend" toward decentralization and "de-massification" described by such writers as John Naisbitt and Alvin Toffler. But if these trends are to reach full flower, much depends on individual initiative, wisdom, and ethical values. In a similar discussion, Nobel Laureate Herb Simon has used the image of a forest ranger alone in the forest. The forest ranger is completely on his own, and "free." Yet by virtue of his superb training he embodies all that is best of the discipline, expertise, and ideals of the Forestry Service.

In science and technology, advanced computing need not be a force for unimaginative conformity; rather, it can offer creative stimulus by enormously enhancing the power to test ideas rapidly at all levels of the research and development process. In the office, factory, and marketplace, the trends are toward a richer diversity of work, products, and services. And in the relationship between the citizen and his government, modern computing has given Little Brother new tools for giving Big Brother as good he gets. In every case, the most fruitful activity lies in devising "loose structures" that preserve diversity, innovation, entrepreneurship, and vitality.

Our culture is following computing technology toward greater decentralization and diversity. How far these trends will develop still depends heavily on the social and cultural structures that are evolving to support the technology. The trends are not inevitable. Authority-loving groups in the Soviet Union, for example, might use computing mainly to aid centralization. Individualistic, undisciplined

Americans might exploit computing mainly to promote their "own thing." Meanwhile the Japanese might achieve a happy medium. As we celebrate Columbia's magnificent new Computer Science Building, let me close by urging that the faculty and students who work there devote no small part of their effort to finding that happy medium. This is no less worthy a goal than advancing scientific and engineering knowledge.

5. Toward the Domestication of Computers

JOEL S. BIRNBAUM

5. Toward the Domestication of Computers*

JOEL S. BIRNBAUM

The rapid evolution and domestication of computer technology and software programs are bringing to more and more people ever-easier access to new and powerful tools that can enrich our daily living and enhance our opportunities for personal creativity and communication.

The Evolution of Pervasive Technologies

AMONG THE ANCIENT RECORDS of human life we find almost 5000-year-old reports of the domestication of dogs in Egypt. Pictures of horses drawing vehicles some 3500 years ago have survived. Man's ability to tame wild creatures and to use them as beasts of burden and providers of food, clothing, and companionship was a critical step in the evolution of civilization. As man learned to domesticate animals, he also learned to modify them—that is, to create breeds better suited for his purposes. The first known treatise on horse breeding and training is over 3000 years old. The horse of today is significantly different from that early

*The notion of domesticating computers is due to my colleague Egon Loebner, and I am grateful to him and to John Doyle for many of the ideas presented.

animal, and the same is true for chickens, cattle, sheep and many of the other creatures closely associated with man.

There are today more computers than people in the United States, and microcomputers are now being manufactured at a rate of more than one million per day. American society has progressed to the point where some citizens will soon own more computing power than the amount projected 30 years ago as the national requirement. Inexorably, the computer technology developed in our laboratories has permeated our offices, our factories, our schools, and now, it would appear, is about to invade our homes. The root of the word "domesticate" relates to suitability to reside in the home, and, therefore, it is reasonable to question the level of domestication of these computers and whether they should be bred to improve their usefulness for that environment. It is also reasonable to ask, and many already have, whether we want them in our lives at all, and whether computer technology can really be used to increase the welfare of the population it serves.

I will try to convince you that while computers are still far from domesticated, there is every indication that they will become so in the next 10 years. Selective breeding must now begin in earnest. The result, if we don't bungle it, will profoundly and positively affect the style and quality of our lives. I will take the somewhat heretical point of view, at least for a computer scientist, that much of the general distaste for today's computers and the fear of their dehumanizing effects on our society is deserved, and that we, the computer scientists, are the culprits. We must now take the lead in rethinking many of the assumptions inherent in personal computer design and application.

In spite of the vast numbers of computers now in use, they are still far from pervasive. Virtually all the pervasive technologies I can think of have passed through four evolutionary stages. Such technologies usually begin as an experimental rarity, a laboratory curiosity, sometimes an accidental discovery in the pursuit of basic science, but much more often they are the result of an entrepreneurial attempt to exploit a perceived opportunity. The second stage of evolution is usually that of an exotic tool or toy, often solving only a cross-section of a problem and used primarily by a narrow class of experts. In the third stage the technology evolves to the point where it is manufactured in quantity, becomes well known and commonplace, but is used directly by only a rather small portion of the population. In the fourth and final stage the technology becomes part of the fabric and infrastructure of life. Its absence is then more noticeable than its presence. For example, a home or a modern hotel room without a color television set is unusual today since we are in the fourth stage of television technology. Contrast this with the third stage some 30 years ago when neighbors would congregate at a pioneer owner's home or in the streets outside store windows to watch the World Series or the Milton Berle Show on the black and white screens of that day. During the third stage of a new technology, there is usually a proliferation of companies seeking an early competitive edge. Product distinctions are clear although there are many lookalikes, and pricing is somewhat arbitrary. A characteristic of the fourth stage is that the businesses consolidate, major innovations are far more difficult because of large in-place investments, and prices stabilize. For example, the 1100 or so American car companies of the third stage have now become four, and prices of comparable (and very similar) models are exceedingly competitive. Personal computer technology today is in stage three, and we can confidently predict that the several hundred personal computer companies vying today for a share of this rapidly expanding market will shrink to a number about 100 times smaller, and that the large dynamic range now seen in software pricing, for example, will soon reach a more rational equilibrium between cost and price.

Many studies have been made of technological evolution, and while we tend to think of it as continuous, in fact it proceeds in fits and starts. Social and economic events, such as wars and depressions, as well as major technical innovations can produce an acceleration or deceleration in the rate of change of the substitution of a new technology for an old for a while, but then the original pattern is resumed. It doesn't seem to matter much what these technologies are; once started, the replacement process continues to completion in a strangely predictable way, whether we are talking about the replacement of sailing ships with steamships, the substitution of airline travel for rail travel, or the introduction of plastics for glass in consumer bottles.

The rate of dispersion of a particular technology is controlled by several factors. Probably the strongest force is the development of a community of common interest. For example, the automobile as a technology for personal transportation could not have achieved stage four without the public's support of the development of a highway network. Similarly, the personal computer will require the creation of extensive data networks in order to be considered seriously as an alternative to the mails or the telephone and telegraph systems, and that will require the public's conviction that such networks are worth having.

While the intensity of this common interest is building, invention and entrepreneurship are extremely rapid and exhibit a form of positive feedback in which each advance feeds on those before, often without the underpinnings of fundamental science or understanding. Remember that most of the industrial revolution was based on early theories of electricity, magnetism, and Newtonian mechanics. Quantum mechanics and electrodynamics were not needed or used for this first tier of invention. This has also been the case in computing, where the hazy outlines of theoretical understanding are only now beginning to emerge. It is not obvious that the *ad hoc* inventions of the computer engineers of the 1960s and 1970s have started us on the right evolutionary course for personal computers for the general population, and it is critical that the rapid advances sure to occur as public interest builds have the right starting point. It is not an exaggeration to say that the personal computers of today, while useful, are primitive, unadapted versions of what their domesticated descendants will look like within a few years.

The Taming of Computers

We can think of technologies in a general way as amplifiers of human capabilities. So, for example, the telephone has widened the range of human speech and hearing, the television has expanded the range of our sight, and the automobile has served to increase our speed of foot and our ability to carry weight. The great promise of computing technology is that it will expand human memory, augment human reasoning, and facilitate human communication. If we judge the progress of personal computing by these lofty goals, we will find it embryonic at best.

Consumer appliances in homes today contain many hidden computers, which are frequently used to save the manufacturer money by substituting an easily mass-produced and very reliable electronic component for more expensive and finicky mechanical parts. Sometimes the computer adds additional functions, flexibilty, or ease of use as well. Consider, for example, the features of current microwave ovens, washing machines, sewing machines and video-cassette recorders. In general, this usage of computers has been very successful; many consumer products cost far less today, have enormously more function, and are much easier to use than their premicrocomputer ancestors, but these are hardly the mind-expanding products alluded to before.

Also relatively successful is the use of computers in personal service networks, which we often take largely for granted. We can reserve an airline seat or a hotel room worldwide from a telephone, or get cash issued day or night by an automatic teller. The safety of our transportation system and, indeed, our national defense is inextricably dependent on the networks of hidden computers behind these deceptively simple user functions. However much we have come to rely on these commercial and military services, this is still hardly the stuff of which intellectual revolutions are made.

The important case to consider is an individual using a nonhidden computer in an attempt to expand his mental powers. The average American would as soon program a personal computer in Basic or Pascal as he would climb into a cage with a circus lion. The reason is the same: Neither the computer nor the lion is really tame; they violate the rule of general access required for true domestication, for neither a lion tamer nor a professional programmer qualifies as a paradigm of general society. Even if one were to master the requisite skills, this begs the second major issue: what is to be done with the now domesticated computer if one is not a professional programmer or a hobbyist interested in an exotic electronic pet? I'll come back to this issue later, but first I'd like to consider taming the computer. How will we know when we've done it correctly?

The test I like best is the one proposed by R. M. Pirzig in his book, *Zen and the Art of Motorcycle Maintenance:* "The material objects . . . can't be right or wrong. They don't have any ethical codes to follow except those people give them. The test of the machine is the satisfaction it gives you. There isn't any other test. If the machine produces tranquility, it's right. If it disturbs you, it's wrong until either the machine or your mind is changed." The media are full of unequivocal proofs that we have gotten it all wrong. Timex/Sinclair, in advertising their Model 1000 computer, ran a successful campaign with the slogan "Why spend thousands to find out you hate computing when you can find out for $49.95?" A recent computer book review section in the *San Francisco Chronicle* had an article about computing books for the general population titled "Cyberphobia and how to cope with it." The cover of a national training magazine featured a photograph of an executive cowering before a terminal, a braid of garlic around his neck, and a silver cross held fearfully before him.

Is this all mindless paranoia? I think not. We can gain some insight into why so many people dislike or fear computers by recognizing that many replacement technologies effectively remove one or more components of the in-place technology. For example, the early automobile was called a horseless carriage. It had the attributes of the carriage without the horse and that meant greater speed, greater range, greater convenience, greater power, and eventually, greater reliability. These were good things for most people, but others who liked horses and viewed them as a symbol of a slower, more romantic time, decried the new technology and opposed the odors and noise and danger it introduced. Any time one technology substitutes for another, a sentimental attachment for the technology being replaced is likely to result. Think of the diesel locomotive as a kind of steamless train, or the steamship as a sailing vessel without sails, and then ask what it is that the computer replaces.

Sometimes the computer replaces material objects. For example, we are told that the computer will help produce a more efficient and paperless society; but paper in an office, in books, or as a medium of personal exchange can be portable, beautiful, historic, or individually differentiated to a degree not now possible with electronic media. We gain efficiency but at the expense of aesthetic values and tradition. We substitute regularity for personality, and many users rebel. The office of the future has been a long time coming, and this is one of the reasons.

The other reasons, though, go far deeper than this, for in many applications what we replace with computers are people. We talk of manufacturing robots, and many people think not of the improved output of the factory but of the fact that it will have far fewer workers. An electronic file, simple enough to be used by professionals and powerful enough to coordinate information from many sources, threatens not only the filing cabinet but the filing clerk. A doctor who has devoted decades to learning how to interpret electrocardiograms is not pleased to be told that a computer program capturing the expertise of his colleagues can do the job more rapidly, accurately, and adaptably. He views the computer as a competitor, not an ally.

So the average person begins with a distaste for computers perhaps rooted in sentimentality but more likely the result of the uneasy perception that the machine may in some way be a replacement for those very faculties of mind that distinguish us from the beasts. Science fiction often portrays this outcome in a threatening way, and the computer scientists have produced a guaranteed reinforcement of the malaise by making machines so complicated to understand.

Advertisement of "user-friendly" systems to the contrary, using most personal computers today requires arcane knowledge of specific and unforgiving command sequences. The computers' designs are optimized by engineers for cost and performance and not for natural usage by ordinary people. This means that the machines must be redesigned to be adaptive; that is, the idiosyncrasies of the user must be accommodated in a way that supports his mental abstraction of the process taking place in the machine. Our software today is rude: it does not recognize individuals.

Ease of use, of course, ultimately depends on the programs that specify the machine's actions. A key factor is the degree to which these programs can be made to hide the details of operation from the users. It is one of our popular fantasies that some people can rapidly learn how to use machines no matter how complex they are. Consider James Bond, rushing into the atomic reactor or the space station that he has never seen before, examining the bewildering maze of dials, buttons, and flashing screens, and pressing precisely the right switches in the proper sequence to thwart the villains just as time runs out. We all know that this is science fiction, but we like to think that somehow it should be possible to fathom the inner workings of complex machinery. Designers have not really concentrated on this goal until recently. I believe we are at an inflection point now, for we have finally realized we must optimize the human resource and not the cost/performance of the machines.

Soon computers will handle the complicated control sequences for us; only then will we be able to substitute simple abstractions for specialized knowledge, just as we now do in using many appliances. Consider one-button automatic tuning on a modern television set, for example, compared to the complex set of knobs needed to adjust the hue, intensity, fine tuning, brightness, and contrast on the sets of just a few years ago. It is possible to rent an American automobile of any model, from any manufacturer, and within a few minutes be driving away, having understood the location and function of the controls. Automatic transmission has made it unnecessary for people to understand the detailed workings of a gear box and clutch. The electric starter has produced a crankless horseless carriage, and we no longer think at all about what happens when we turn the ignition key, since automatic choking mechanisms or fuel injection have replaced some of the specific sequences that used to be required. Any user can very rapidly grasp the concept behind a lever labeled "Neutral," "Drive," and "Reverse," or a button labeled "Start." The challenge is to produce this type of mental model to drive the computer systems and then to represent it consistently to the user.

Hiding complexity from the user while retaining a rich function set will require computer programs far more sophisticated than those we now write. The computer power required to execute such programs will be staggering. Simply increasing the speed of a computing cycle and decreasing the cost and access time of memory by advances in hardware technology will fall far short of what is required for this task. Computer scientists must reorganize the internal structure of the computers, modifying their architecture to greatly increase the number of operations that can be carried out in parallel. I think this will lead to computers that are organized as sets of special-purpose processors, each optimized for a particular class of tasks, such as extracting the patterns of speech or handwriting, rapidly searching large data stores, managing the information on a display screen, or doing a particular type of simulation. These will be coordinated by high-performance, mass-produced, yet simple, general-purpose controllers. The programming style will be object-oriented—that is, control will be passed in the form of messages among self-descriptive entities. We will need systems thousands of times more powerful than the primitive general-purpose serial engines of today. Early examples of such machines are now beginning to appear in research laboratories, but their interconnection and coordination involve many unsolved problems.

Software must be designed to optimize not the way machines work, but the way people think; and we can go a long way toward this goal even with our present machines. Integrated programming environments are beginning to mask details from the user and to provide consistent access to services; natural language, touch screens, and speech are being combined to replace and augment the more formalized keyboard interaction. In the new world of domesticated computers, slow, surly, uncooperative software will not survive. As we enter the fourth stage of computer technology, the successful companies will recognize that in a rapidly expanding industry most users are beginners. The cumbersome instruction manuals and training classes of today must give way to an intuitive form of learning by doing the things that seem natural. Today's video-games producers have stumbled onto the right experiential model. Domesticated computers should be self-evident and self-documenting, and they should offer strong positive reinforcement almost immediately. Most users should never need to write a program. Professional computer scientists and programmers will survive, I hope, but increasingly their jobs will be to improve high-performance architectures and interfaces to mask the computer's internal complexity, and to develop tools to help users build and maintain applications.

What Computers Will Do

For now, let us assume that these powerful, domesticated computers exist. The crucial question remains: what will they actually do? How can they increase the capacity of our minds? There are many obvious things such computers will do (could do today, if computer companies were less competitive and could agree on communication standards).

Most of the scenarios the airline magazines and other learned journals are so fond of fall into the "x-of-the-future" category, where x is a factory, an office, a school, or a home. Usually the home is viewed as an extension of the workplace or classroom, or as a candidate for home management services, such as energy control, security, or checkbook balancing, an activity apparently now near the top of the list of America's pressing problems. Let us examine these scenarios a little more closely.

Computers in the workplace today are largely used to perform what I think of as competence functions—tasks that help a person to do his specific job (e.g. an electrical engineer to design circuits, a businessman to analyze a spreadsheet, or a secretary to do word processing). It is relatively easy to measure whether the computers are doing a good job in these activities. The people who use them regard them as essential tools for performing that job and invest in the needed training. We can determine whether the worker's productivity has increased sufficiently, or whether the quality of the output is enough better to merit the expense of the computer system involved.

More interesting are the computer-aided work functions, those core functions most people perform, which are largely independent of industry or profession. These activities can be broken into three related tasks. First is the creation and distribution of "documents" (a generic label for paper documents as well as electronic text/data/voice/image combinations). Here the computer replaces a secretary and a typewriter or a yellow pad and a pencil. The second task is the storage, analysis, and retrieval of information (the computer as a filing clerk, support staff, or research librarian). The third category is user-to-user communication (the computer and communication system replace conventional telephones, telegraphs, or facsimile machines).

Acceptance of these advanced systems has been much slower than predicted, because, I think, they have been hard to use and the functions being replaced have not been significantly improved. This is now changing. The office systems industry is early in stage three now, with inventions coming furiously and huge companies jockeying for position. Electronic mail, with useful store-and-forward capabilities that eliminate the missed phone call and the barriers of international time zones, will be widespread shortly. Soon even the simple home machines using TV sets for displays and telephone lines for communication will have easy access to large and diverse databases—the world's cookbook collection , or ten different articles from ten different encyclopedias on a topic of immediate importance; worldwide local weather or news; repair manuals for discontinued products—a seemingly endless set of attractive global services and information, hard to come by today, selected by simple menu-like commands and purchased on a pay-as-you-go basis. There are few, if any, technical impediments to this vision, and prototype systems have been working for several years now.

When these low-cost combinations of telephone network, television set, and personal computer are complete, I think you will all want them in your homes. They will enable you to send and receive messages instantaneously to and from any connected television set. The world's libraries will be at your disposal, and intelligent, centralized reference services will aid in the collection and updating of information. The spread of cable TV and video disk technology will add color video and sound to these capabilities— imagine a pronouncing dictionary, the Schwann record catalog on demand (we'll be able to compare, for example, different performances of the same piece of music), encyclopedias with film clips instead of still pictures, access to facsimiles of rare documents, and interactive bedtime stories in which children will be able to select their own endings. Driven by the economics of electronic communication, banking, shopping, and publishing, myriad new personal applications as yet unthought of will evolve. Once these services are easy to use from a consistent user interface, they will become the commonplace facilities of stage four. They will not need to be resident on the personal computer itself but will be features provided by the network of information servers. Remember that the technology-substitution process, once started, almost always runs to completion; we have already begun, and so there is little doubt that this will happen. But what of the revolution? These core functions are attractive, but they're really just more efficient substitutes for tasks we can already do.

Software as a Medium

In 1785, four years before he was guillotined, Antoine Lavoisier, the father of modern chemistry, reflected on the fact that his discovery of the true nature of combustion, which disproved the century-old phlogiston theory, was vigorously opposed by many of the most eminent scientists of that day. Ironically, one of the greatest critics of Lavoisier's work was Joseph Priestley, the distinguished discoverer of oxygen, who held that a colorless, odorless, tasteless substance, phlogiston, was the key ingredient of all combustible substances. After combustion, the phlogiston would be liberated to the air and only the true substance, the ash, would remain. Lavoisier took a philosophical view towards the illogical opposition to his conclusive experiments. He said, "I do not expect my ideas to be adopted all at once. The human mind gets creased into a way of seeing things. Those who have envisaged nature according to a certain point of view during much of their careers, rise only with difficulty to new ideas. It is the passage of time, therefore, that must confirm and destroy the opinions I have presented. Meanwhile, I observe with great satisfaction that the young people are beginning to study this science without prejudice."

My greatest satisfaction today comes not from the bankbookless banking, the postmanless mail, and the other y-less x replacements I have alluded to, but from a groundswell of personal computer–based creativity that is now beginning. Not surprisingly, this uncreasing of the mind is being led by our young people and has nothing to do with balancing checkbooks or updating the home recipe file. The evidence is all around us, but because much of it is now directed at the largely mindless video game market, it is perhaps hidden from the general adult view.

Software is emerging as a medium, a unique medium, a very hot, interactive medium. A culture of media stars is developing—teenagers and college students who sign their programs, who have a following, who hire software agents to represent them. The programs are beginning to be distributed by publishers in bookstores, including some of our oldest and most respected book publishing firms. Genius programmers appear on TV talk shows. There is a software top-ten bestseller list, and subindustries like software distribution and software packaging have emerged. The comparisons with the record and book industries are obvious. Issues of piracy, copyright, and compatibility are already troublesome. Software review magazines have appeared, and a *Whole Earth Software Catalog* is being published. Mass distributions of programs like *VisiCalc* and *WordStar*, business bestsellers, or *Pac-man* and its thousand lookalikes are a billion dollar business today. Within this framework a new type of literature is being written. Some have called it the literature of the future, and I am sure the scholars in the audience are waiting with bated breath for my critical comparison of *Ulysses* and *Donkey Kong*.

This attitude misses the point entirely. Software and literature are alike only in that they are both media to present and share views publicly. Literature and television and hi-fi are passive, cool, static, one-way broadcasts. They evolved from the technology available at the time of their conception. Software is hot, interactive, dynamic. It is unlike anything we have seen before in its ability to draw people into the environment it creates. It is expressive, but for now it can only be manipulated by a few media stars. Computer science's principal task in this decade will be to provide the tools to eliminate this barrier, and once we have done this I believe a flood of creativity will occur. It will come mostly from the large grass-roots population now excluded from such interaction. Interacting with the new software will be as different from watching TV or doing word processing or reserving hotel rooms electronically as can be imagined. We will need a new verb to describe it. We have seen only the pop music side of the medium so far—the classical versions are coming now, and they are not going to be aimed at developing the hand-eye coordination necessary to repel an alien invasion.

Let me give you some early examples of the work of the media stars. A bestselling program, *Typing Master,* available now for home computers, analyzes the user's performance on typing assignments and provides immediate feedback on specific improvements. Even lifelong professional typists learn immediately and interactively how to improve their speed and accuracy. The extension to many other skills is obvious. One-chip signal processors will permit biofeedback to people learning to sing or to play musical instruments, helping with the difficult-to-teach relationships between anatomical control and auditory phenomena. We will be able to see on a screen in real time the spectrum of the sounds produced. The visual feedback of auditory phenomena will show dynamically the relation of the harmonics to the fundamental, for example, in a way our ears cannot do. It will enable singers and musicians to compare sound patterns and rhythms with stored templates produced by master musicians or with their own earlier efforts. Programs to analyze speech accents and cadences are further in the future but certainly possible. The same techniques with different sensors will permit the semiautomatic tuning of instruments like pianos and Porsches.

Another type of personal computer program now starting to appear is the kit, like the *Pinball Construction Set.* Using simple pictorial interfaces and pointers, objects (in this case flippers, bumpers, spinners, bonus lights, etc.) are selected from a pictorial menu, moved about on a screen, and assembled according to the rules previously imbedded in the pinball program by the professional programmer. Many parameters in the pinball program can be changed—the location and elasticity of the bumpers and flippers, bonus point combinations, etc. Items difficult to change on real pinball machines could also be modifiable: nonphysical gravitational fields, ball cross-section, etc. After the almost infinitely variable game has been designed by the user *without writing a single line of code,* it can be played immediately and further modified. The output of the program is the pinball game. Future versions of this idea include a music construction kit. The objects now are notes, score markings, tempi, etc. We can create melodies, snip them with iconic scissors, combine them with preprogrammed melodies, transpose to new keys, and so forth, with no user programming. The application is music composition, and the output of the program will be the score of the music itself. We will be able to play the results on conventional instruments if we desire.

This entire notion of kits seems to me a very powerful one. If the appropriate sets of rules of combination, the constraints, can be imbedded in the machine by experts, then design can become possible based only on function and aesthetics for a vastly greater proportion of our population than is now possible. Consider an amateur architect designing an addition to his house using such techniques. The cost, the structural factors for different materials, and the connection rules for electrical and plumbing fixtures will be preprogrammed, and the computer will monitor these constraints, physical or economic, as the design is produced. Cost estimates, blueprints, and material lists will be the output. Professional mechanical and electrical engineers and architects are already using early versions of such tools. In ten years, I think there will be hundreds of variations available for everything from landscape architecture to cash management, enabling people to concentrate on the design instead of the routine drudgery. "Computer-aided design" will be an important new way of solving problems in all fields.

The area of computer-aided education will also explode soon, I think. The new programs will depart from the stylized programmed instruction and boring drill that dominate the field today. One existing program that I like introduces people to the workings of a computer by having a pictorial repairman scurry about a representation of a computer's innards much in the style of a computer game. The repairman must deal with the hazards of static charges, voltage surges, and other real-world phenomena as he analyzes symptoms and makes tests to find the trouble. The user learns about the machine experientially: he becomes familiar with the nomenclature and basic functional characteristics of major components by interacting with them. He learns which measurements to make to diagnose a failure, which parts to replace, and so on.

This type of videogame, like the early sword and sorcerer games such as *Adventure,* contains a world model and basic reasoning capability. The computer, in a sense, is a type of expert, combining analytic and heuristic information. This, of course, represents the great promise of artificial intelligence technology. We can think of a calculator as an arithmetic apprentice and be confident that soon personal algebra helpers will be commonplace. We can now purchase spelling assistants, and one day grammar tutors will appear, to help us with the mechanical tasks of writing so that we can concentrate our energies on thinking and style. Many companies are now working on these knowledge-based expert systems; they will be used to fix machines, to help diagnose illness, to translate languages, to locate oil, and they will help to codify human wisdom so that knowledge becomes reusable across a wide range of only superficially different problems.

Within a few years this kind of technology will be practical on home computers. It will, for example, enable personalized filters to eliminate electronic junk mail and sort the remainder according to content and priority. We will see a greatly enhanced ability to search global data bases without providing detailed parameters for the search. Cottage industries will arise that will permit creative people to sell poems or concerti or statistics to an electronic mailing list of people who have indicated similar interests (often without a publisher as intermediary). Early versions of every application I have mentioned are operational today, and I think the evolution from these prototypes will be rapid.

The Domesticated Computer

When I was studying to be an engineer, I used to think how wonderful it would have been to live during the last 30 years of the nineteenth century, when the great inventions of the industrial revolution were appearing at a dizzying rate. Later, when I studied physics, I regretted not living in the period of the great discoveries of relativity and quantum mechanics. I have now changed my mind. I am glad that I am around now, because I think that the next ten years will be more exciting than any period we have ever seen, because so many more people will participate in the invention process. We have at last arrived at an understanding of the real potential of computer technology. We are finally concentrating on the right problem—making computers usable by everyone. Computers, long pilloried as a dehumanizing force, will become the most powerful means of personal creative expression and communication ever known.

I have talked a lot about the domestication of computers and what I think that could come to mean. I would like to end by quoting a short passage from *The Little Prince*, by Antoine de Saint Exupéry. In that book, you may remember, the Little Prince, in love with what he thinks is a unique flower on his tiny planet, but exasperated by her pettiness and idiosyncrasies, has wandered from asteroid to asteroid observing the strange ways of men. At last he reaches Earth where he is dismayed to learn that his flower is nothing more than a common rose and that he has wasted so much time catering to her whims. He is disconsolate when, in a vast desert, he meets a wild fox. The fox says to the Little Prince, "'To me, you are still nothing more than a little boy who is just like a hundred thousand other little boys, and I have no need of you, and you, on your part, have no need of me. To you I am nothing more than a fox, like a hundred thousand other foxes, but if you tame me, then we shall need each other. To me you will be unique in all the world. To you I shall be unique in all the world. One only understands the things that one tames . . . you become responsible, forever, for what you have tamed. . . . If you want a friend, tame me . . .'" Later, after the Little Prince has tamed the fox, they come to a sad farewell. "'Goodbye,' said the fox, 'and now here is my secret—a very simple secret. It is only with the heart that one can see rightly. What is essential is invisible to the eye. . . . It is the time you have wasted for your rose that makes your rose so important.'"

The fox has given you my prescription for domesticating computers: our success should be measured by how much we come to care about them. I hope that this splendid new center at Columbia will produce people and ideas that make us care very much indeed.

6. Planning New Ventures in the University

PETER LIKINS

6. Planning New Ventures in the University

PETER LIKINS

An active participant in the implementation of organizational change in several major universities, Dr. Likins recounts the special story of the Computer Science Department at Columbia University ("a textbook case") and formulates lightheartedly some first principles for success in academic planning and reorganization.

IT'S A SPECIAL SOURCE of pride and pleasure for me to participate in the celebration of the entry into adulthood of a child I helped to create. There are few experiences in life that can match the pleasures and the pain of raising children, but bringing a computer science department to life comes close.

Like my own father, I've watched from afar as this creature of my passion, this computer science department, grew to maturity and achievement, so I can take a measure of satisfaction from that success, as perhaps my father does from my own.

It came as a great surprise to me that I was swept away from Columbia before this department had a chance to grow up. I was perhaps the last to see what others saw immediately in predicting my future. I was the last to realize that *short people make good presidents*. The reason, of course,

99

is simple: *short people are the last to know it's raining*. This is important in the field of higher education, where it rains a lot. Sometimes it's easier to remain optimistic and enthusiastic if you don't know it's raining, and success in this business *requires* optimism and enthusiasm.

Success in my business also requires a sense of balance, and a capacity for humor. A university president must find exactly the right amount of humor in this saying: "It was not the pear on the tree that caused all the trouble in the Garden of Eden, it was the apple on the ground."

Let's pause to consider the elements of a successful new venture in the university. What does it take to bring about change in a university? What distinguishes a successful initiative from a failed idea? How can we ensure that a meteoric success will not, like the meteor, fade rapidly into obscurity, but instead endure as a permanent part of the university, which is an institution quintessentially committed to the concept of permanence?

Before I go too far I should acknowledge that I don't know the answers to these questions. Learning to live with questions I can't answer definitively has been hard for me as an engineer, but it is a lesson I have had to learn in order to do my job. A fine young assistant professor of philosophy told me when I was a freshman at Stanford 30 years ago that I should give up my plans to be an engineer because any discipline for which questions had definitive answers would eventually prove insufficient to my needs; and 25 years later I began to suspect that he was right. Whether right or wrong, his arguments foreshadowed my own first principle of academic planning:

> *1st Law: Initiate new ventures at an early stage of their evolution in your mind; don't wait until you're so sure of your position that you can't be persuaded to change it.*

The engineering professor in me rebels at these words. Whereas once upon a time I stood before others to speak only when I had something to say that was verifiable but not obvious, now I am presuming to address a very distinguished assembly to say what is perhaps obvious but not verifiable.

If there is a first principle of academic planning, then there must be a second principle. Mine goes like this:

> *2nd Law: The university is a second-order viscoelastic medium; forces generated in response to change include a vanishingly small opposing component proportional to the magnitude of the change, a somewhat larger opposing component proportional to the* rate *of change, and a very large component proportional to the* acceleration *of change, of unknown but invariably perverse direction.*

As an admonition, the second principle suggests that if we introduce change with low acceleration, then we may accomplish substantial change and eventually quite rapid change safely; sudden changes, on the other hand, have large and unpredictable consequences even if the changes intended are small. In other words, jerking people around is dangerous. That should be pretty obvious, but the landscape is strewn with the remains of academic administrators who ignored the second principle.

Another way to think about the university is by means of the fabric analogy. You can stretch and shape the fabric to your will if you do the job with your ears cocked, alert to the first sound of tearing. When you hear that ominous ripping sound you needn't stop, but you must slow down or the integrity of the fabric may be destroyed. If you don't ease back, you may get the fabric into the desired shape, but it will have a big hole it it.

Principles 1 and 2 both offer the same advice to an academic administrator eager for change: learn to listen to people. It turns out that most people in a university are pretty smart. Isn't *that* a surprising conclusion?

These principles also argue for a mentality that is fundamentally comfortable with change. New ventures should be explored easily and frequently, without traumatizing commitment to specific results and without undue haste or impatience.

There is a third principle, a third law, but it's not mine. I'll call this Walt Whitman's principle of academic administration, because I've purloined it from his collected works:

3rd Law: "It is provided in the essence of things from any fruition of success, no matter what, shall come forth something to make a greater struggle necessary."

Success brings its own problems. If you don't enjoy solving further problems, you should avoid solving the first. There are two ways to avoid the consequences of successful problem solving, but only one is acceptable in the university environment.

The first option, of course, is to duck problems whenever possible and then to confront unavoidable problems grudgingly and fail to solve them. This option leads to a reputation among colleagues for laziness and cowardice.

The second and preferable alternative is one that Julian Cole, my department chairman of long ago, called *dynamic incompetence*. The practitioners of dynamic incompetence eagerly volunteer for onerous duty and then fail miserably, assuring that they will forever after be excused and even avoided as problem solvers.

Those of us who feel compelled to solve organizational and administrative problems in the university are doomed by Whitman's principle to deal with the proliferation of problems that come in the wake of every success. Whitman's principle hooks us all and transforms perfectly good professors into administrators.

Because my training is in Newtonian Mechanics, I am permitted no more than three fundamental principles or laws. This is unfortunate, because I really wish I could espouse three more laws, as follows:

4th Law: A little bit of money helps a little bit; a lot of money helps a lot.

5th Law: Never bet on a horse without a jockey.

6th Law: Don't take yourself too seriously.

This concludes the theoretical part of my lecture; what remains are merely illustrative examples.

When I came to Columbia in 1976 I discovered in the first millisecond that we had a problem in computer science. Solving the problem took a whole lot longer.

When I moved to Lehigh in 1982 I was told immediately that the Lehigh problem in computer science was essentially the same as the old Columbia problem, and it was the hope that I would recreate the miracle of Columbia computer science. After a year on the job I am convinced that the solutions must be different in these two institutions even if the problems are similar. We've made some decisions at Lehigh that the Board approved only three days ago, but it's too soon to judge the outcome. Principles 2, 4, and 5 tell me that I still have cause for concern at Lehigh; this problem may not yet be solved. In the words of Yogi Berra, we might be making the wrong mistake. Only time will tell.

In 1976 Columbia had not one computer science faculty but two, with one in Engineering and the other in Arts and Sciences. In 1982 Lehigh had exactly the same situation. In both institutions it seemed obvious to everyone that the status quo was grossly unsatisfactory, but both situations had nonetheless endured for years of debilitating strife.

How well I remember when Omar Wing, as chairman of Columbia's Electrical Engineering and Computer Science Department, returned from a faculty recruiting trip to California with the news that the competing Columbia Computing Science group in Arts and Sciences had just completed the same circuit. Needless to say, no bright young Ph.D.'s from Stanford or Berkeley expressed interest in coming to Columbia that year to get caught in the squeeze play. We were completely paralyzed by our organizational structure.

The need for change in organizational structure in the university is most often a need to break up the existing structure, removing obstacles to the good work of the faculty. When this is the case, the premium is on action leading to change, and the specific outcome matters less than the fact of change. The role of the administrator is to initiate change, to precipitate change, and then to work with the faculty to search out the best achievable outcome.

Professors, and especially engineering professors, usually find workable solutions to organizational problems once they accept the responsibility to do so, but it is rare for the faculty to *initiate* organizational change. If the initiative for change doesn't come from the nominal leader of the organization, the status quo will prevail, and sometimes it takes an incredibly energetic push just to get the organization off dead center. Despite all the talk about the liberal inclinations in the university, we are astonishingly conservative in organizational terms. We are remarkably resistant to the kind of adaptation to the external environment that preoccupied Charles Darwin, and we may yet pay the price that concerned him.

When I came to the Columbia School of Engineering and Applied Science in 1976, a stranger to the place, a 39-year-old UCLA professor whose California origins were probably a bit suspect in New York, I could see almost immediately that some kind of major organizational shake-up would be helpful in breaking the faculty's internal stalemate. I knew that I couldn't do anything until I had earned the confidence of the faculty, so I deliberately waited an entire year before I began acting like a revolutionary.

During my first year at Columbia I soaked up the culture of this remarkable institution and worked hard to earn the respect of the distinguished faculty. Some of my colleagues were worried about my capacity to survive and serve their interests in the fierce political environment at Columbia. They were afraid I would be eaten alive by the powerful deans in Arts and Sciences, who by reputation in my school ate engineers for breakfast. Although in six years at Columbia I never saw a single powerful ogre anywhere in the administration, I learned in that first year that I had some faculty anxieties to dispel.

As my second year in the deanship at Columbia dawned, I concocted a scheme for completely reorganizing the academic departments in the school and began a process of one-on-one faculty consultation that occupied an entire year, including every tenured member of the engineering faculty on campus, all of the nontenured faculty in certain key departments, and senior faculty in related disciplines all over the university. I don't remember now what I proposed originally, but I considered the mergers of Industrial with Mechanical Engineering, and Chemical Engineering with Mining, Metallurgical and Mineral Engineering. I suggested a new Department of Computer Science and Operations Research, moving the latter from Civil Engineering and Engineering Mechanics and the former from Electrical Engineering and Computer Science.

Although I didn't commit myself irrevocably to any single plan, I certainly caught the interest of the faculty and created an environment in which some kind of change was anticipated. Following the first and second principles, I listened to the faculty's alternatives, let the ideas ferment, and pressed persistently but not violently for a realignment of the faculty. The plan that emerged at the end of a year of negotiations bore little resemblance to my initial proposal, but it had the support of the faculty. It realigned personnel in four of the six departments, and introduced two new ones, including Computer Science.

I remember well a critical faculty meeting in which the reorganization was discussed. I even recall a comment from a professor destined for the new Computer Science Department, whose words made me believe that my investment of the first year in earning the confidence of the faculty had paid off. "We've had bitter experience with a dean who was strong but not honest," he said "and we've had sad experience with a dean who was honest but not strong. Now we have a dean who is both honest and strong, and we'd be wise to support his plan."

But I must not forget the 4th and 5th laws of academic administration:

I'm sure that most of you remember them well, but I'll repeat myself for those of you who had wine with your lunch.

4th Law: A little bit of money helps a little bit; a lot of money helps a lot.

5th Law: Never bet on a horse without a jockey.

Shortly after I came to Columbia, I spoke to Tom Horton, IBM's university relations officer, about my hope that IBM would help me to strengthen Computer Science in the Engineering School at Columbia. He laughed and told me that Computer Science at Columbia was an organizational mess; but he also promised to try to help me financially if I could solve the organizational problems. "Get your house in order," he said, "and then come back to me." I left his office satisfied, knowing that a little bit of money would help a little bit.

And then dear Mrs. Hudson died and left Columbia a lot of money, the largest bequest in university history, controlled by the president but properly belonging to the School of Engineering and Applied Science. President McGill agreed to permit me to commit the money under two conditions: the Hudson bequest had to be used first to pay off millions of dollars in internal debt and second for new initiatives. With the new departments in prospect but not yet approved, we hoped to be ready for the new initiatives. Eventually we established the Hudson Chair in which Dean Gross now sits, setting up the Applied Physics and Nuclear Engineering Department under his chairmanship. By augmenting a small sum from the widow of Edwin Howard Armstong, we also established the Armstrong Chair in which Joe Traub now sits. We set up a war chest for computer science and allowed ourselves to think in ambitious terms about the future. At this critical juncture, we received an extremely important boost from Norman Mintz in the Provost's Office. Norman committed a million dollars from the Levi bequest to our arsenal, and we had another Chair. Equally important was our sense that he believed in our ability to make this venture succeed.

We accelerated our discussions with the young Computing Science faculty in Arts and Sciences, and with Dean Fraenkel and other senior faculty. Dean Fraenkel was supportive of anything that brought quality and intellectual distinction to Columbia. We concentrated on obeying the 5th law: *never bet on a horse without a jockey.*

I first met Joe Traub in Berkeley, where he was on

sabbatical from his chairmanship at Carnegie-Mellon University. I approached him initially for advice, but he must have known as I did that I hoped for more. In the months that followed I was a persistent suitor, and Joe remained chaste and cautious. My organization was not yet set, and he didn't know how we would treat computer science organizationally at Columbia. The Computing Science faculty in Arts and Sciences were anxious to have Joe come to us to lead a new computer science department, and those in Electrical Engineering and Computer Science wanted Joe and others to join their department. These discussions required a great deal of time and patience on all sides.

Joe talked to our president, Bill McGill, at a party at Mal Teich's apartment in the village, and he talked to Tom Horton to test the commitment at IBM. Tom promised to get me in to see Mr. Cary, then CEO, if Joe joined us at Columbia and we merged the two faculty groups into one department.

I talked to Pamela McCorduck, Joe's wife, about her own professional opportunities in New York, and I'm pleased to see that my confidence in her future as a New York writer is being justified.

Gradually we came together, and the Computer Science Department at Columbia was born, with Joe Traub as its founding Chairman and IBM support augmenting the Hudson money. Our venture was launched.

I've played a role in many new ventures in the university, at UCLA, Columbia, and Lehigh, but the story of computer science at Columbia is the only one that reads like a textbook case. And even this story cannot be told triumphantly too soon, because the university loves permanent achievement, established over time. The Computer Science Department at Columbia is still young, and you have promises to keep, and miles to go before you sleep.

7. University-Industry Partnership in Computer Science

LEWIS M. BRANSCOMB

7. University-Industry Partnership in Computer Science

LEWIS M. BRANSCOMB

After briefly reviewing some of the highlights of IBM's 25-year-long relationship with Columbia University, Dr. Branscomb surveys current trends in education, science, and technology, showing how deeply rooted and vital to continuing progress university-industry interaction and cooperation have become.

IBM and Columbia University

IBM AND THIS UNIVERSITY have had a long and special relationship that goes back at least 55 years and has few, if any, counterparts. It is still very much alive.

One might say that IBM's relationship with science began here in 1928 when the ideas of Benjamin Wood—then head of Columbia's Collegiate Educational Research—about the potential use of machines in education persuaded Thomas J. Watson, Senior, to have three truckloads of tabulating, card punching, and sorting equipment dispatched to the basement of Hamilton Hall.

The work that was done with those machines represented perhaps the earliest use of technology to permit a substantial reform in precollege education in this country. For, until then, no one had been capable of the large-scale test scoring

111

and analysis necessary to assert discipline on school quality.

Seeing these machines at work, a young Columbia astronomer named Wallace Eckert began to speculate on how they could speed up his own work in refining the calculations of lunar and planetary orbits. Eckert, having learned of Mr. Watson's interest in the use of machines for educational and scientific purposes, proceeded to draw up a list of equipment needed to create the kind of laboratory he envisioned.

The time was 1933—the bottom of the Depression. Nevertheless, Mr. Watson again gave the go-ahead, and Eckert's new laboratory—the only one of its kind in the world— opened the following year under the aegis of Columbia's Astronomy Department. By the late 1930s, the attic of Pupin Hall had become a crossroads for visiting scientists from all over the world.

In the mid-1940s, with developments in computing coming rapidly, IBM began to build up its own scientific capability.

Eckert, meanwhile, had joined the Naval Observatory to mechanize the Nautical Almanac and print error-free tables of the lunar ephemeris for use in navigation. In 1945, however, he accepted Mr. Watson's invitation to become director of IBM's new Department of Pure Science and to organize a joint IBM-Columbia laboratory on the Columbia campus. The lab would "serve as a world center for the treatment of problems in various fields of science, whose solution depends on the effective use of applied mathematics and mechanical calculations."

The Watson Lab at Columbia

For the next 25 years, until its activities were transferred to our nearby and growing research center in Yorktown Heights, a remarkable range of professional interests were pursued here at the Watson Scientific Computing Laboratory at Columbia University.

The Naval Ordinance Research Calculator, or NORC—the most powerful computer of its time, and so advanced that it remained in productive operation for 13 years—was designed and built here.

As the laboratory's emphasis shifted to solid-state electronics and then to life sciences:

- The Michelson-Morley experiment was repeated and improved by two orders of magnitude using the newly developed ammonia maser.
- Attempts were made to grow diamonds.
- Investigators sought to store information in nuclear magnetic resonance. (I understand that in those days a popular source of protons for NMR experiments was Wildroot Cream Oil hair tonic.)
- Researchers probed the mechanism of photosynthesis.
- The behavior of matter near absolute zero was studied.
- And the relationship between structure and function of many metal-containing proteins and enzymes was investigated.

For IBM, the Watson Laboratory at Columbia afforded a window on the academic world, where educators and scientists worked in fields that offered interesting possibilities for the use of calculating machines and, later, computers. For the university, the liaison provided convenient access for students to teaching in areas not spanned by the existing academic departments and enabled students and faculty to do research in these areas.

In many ways, this 25-year joint IBM-Columbia activity anticipated relationships that are now becoming ever more important to industry and universities alike.

Universities as Trend-Setters

Research departments of computer science, electrical engineering, and materials science have now matured technologically to the point where universities are not only the source of many new ideas but are also eager to be the proving ground for new systems concepts. In their role as sophisticated leading-edge users of information technology, universities and the scientific community have been driving revolutions in computing style for a number of years.

During the 1970s, for example, time-shared minicomputers were adapted to serve the needs of department-level organizations in universities and research laboratories, where they are still popular. Universities also became the leading designers and users of heterogeneous networks and interactive languages.

The news is that academic/scientific computing requirements increasingly coincide with those of *any* professional end user. We therefore see new modes of integration and community between the scientific and commercial camps of computing.

Trend: Professional Workstations

Everyone knows how the enormous popularity of the microcomputer system has decentralized the control of information assets right down to the individual. It has shifted the emphasis from accessing information created by others to the creation of information and documents under the individual's control.

The continuation of our industry's extraordinary progress in reducing the cost and increasing the speed of logic and memory now puts in the hands of individual professionals of all kinds computer power that previously had to be shared.

The one disadvantage of the standalone personal computer is its isolation from central sources of information and communications to which the individual needs easy access. In addition, economies of scale still encourage sharing of certain facilities. Good examples are disk storage and high-quality, all-points-addressable printers.

Trend: Local Area Communications

For the solutions to these problems, the personal computer user must look to new capabilities in local area networks, which must also provide day-to-day communications among professionals, linking personal workstations, shared institutional data, and shared storage and output facilities.

For the last decade, commercial customers have presented the most demanding requirements for networks. Commercial enterprises are run on high-speed, high-availability transaction networks with stringent requirements for data integrity. Now, however, the universities are driving the innovative trends in the use of local area networks with large numbers of intelligent workstations.

You are probably aware, for example, of IBM's collaborative project with Carnegie-Mellon University. Like most universities, Carnegie-Mellon seeks the full integration of computing into undergraduate and graduate education. By the end of the decade, the school expects to provide all of its 5,500 students, faculty, researchers, and professional staff with access to computer workstations at least an order of magnitude more powerful than today's home computers. Each will also have access to shared, central data bases and to other workstations through a high-speed local area network.

Many other U.S. universities are laying plans for such networks, as well. What these universities are exploring may well become the wave of the future for the commercial world, too—especially in any large organization that prefers to operate in a heavily decentralized and highly creative mode. That is the nature of a good university, and I believe it will become the nature of many commercial and public institutions in the future.

Trend: Large-Scale Computing in Business

Very-large-scale computing now enjoys an accelerating growth in industry as well as science. Demand on the computer power of the data processing facilities of our largest customers is growing at 40 to 60% per year, compounded.

The explosion of microcomputers among the nation's work force means more workload, not less, for central computing facilities. Penetration—that is, increasing the ratio of workstations to employees, which is proceeding apace—is only part of this equation. The development of powerful, 3-to 5-MIP (million instructions per second) workstations will increase, not decrease, the workload on central CPUs for several reasons.

For one thing, users accustomed to getting spreadsheets, color graphics, windowing, and so on on a standalone personal computer will demand more complex information from central data bases to take advantage of these capabilities. Additional workload will result from the larger transactions (requiring more data) that are possible with more powerful terminals.

Still more computer power will be needed to meet the rapidly growing requirement for fractional-second machine response times, which greatly leverage end-user productivity.

The strongest trend, however, is the tremendous growth of end-user interactive computing, dependent on institutional data collection and made more rewarding for end users by the power of personal workstations.

Commercial computing divides roughly into three areas: batch, data base/data communications (or transaction) computing, and end-user interactive computing—by which I mean the whole range of applications from business graphics to programming development and engineering design. Ten years ago, batch processing dominated; on-line data base/data communications applications (like airline reservations and banking transactions) accounted for some 20% of the installed computer workload, and end-user interactive computing was an insignificant factor. In the late 1970s, however, the combination of on-line data base/data communications activity and emerging end-user interactive workloads began to exceed batch processing. This was especially significant because these power-consuming forms of computing could not be spread across three shifts of work as batch jobs could. The capacity all had to be available during regular working hours, when the users needed the information.

Today, with interactive computing (which uses even more computer power than data base/data communications applications) growing at 60% a year, the logarithmic curve of computer power installed in the central facilities of large corporations has turned upward once again, and the high-end computer business—far from being mature—is more dynamic than ever.

Ask any of the traditional Harvard Business School questions that seek to classify the phase a business is in—from entrepreneurial birth, to maturity and decline—and you will discover that production of large mainframes is still a young and vital industry whose potential is limited only by its ability to keep delivering better price-performance ratios in its products, year in and year out.

Thus, despite our fascination with the extraordinary revolution in individual workstations, predictions that the big central computer will become a dinosaur are premature.

Explosion in Supercomputing

In the scientific world, supercomputing seems on the verge of an explosion of applications variety.

Previously, the hydrodynamicists and aeronautical experts, the weather and climate modelers, and the oil exploration geophysicists were typical users of the largest computing equipment available. They used these machines to get more accurate answers from well-known and well-verified systems of equations.

Today, however, there is increasing conviction that large-scale computation can be used to discover, for example, new principles of nature, becoming the scientist's collaborator and not just his data-reduction technician. This is a turn-around in the point of view expressed in 1973 at a conference on this subject at the Institute for Advanced Studies, which concluded that the computer had not been primarily responsible for any new ideas.

If this trend continues, a growing fraction of the scientific community will need at least occasional access to the largest computing facilities that can be produced. Consequently, we see intense development of special purpose architectures, usually for powerful machines, generically referred to as supercomputers and usually for scientific use. It is interesting to observe, however, that the first Cray X-MP machine was delivered to Digital Productions, Inc. to help with the production of animated movies.

Many other forms of special purpose machines will arise out of the new research in systems architecture. One example is IBM's Yorktown Simulation Engine, structured as a 256-way multiprocessor for design automation. The same principle can now be found in commercial products—basically workstations containing powerful multiprocessor architectures for simulating circuit designs.

An enormous potential for systems research results from these two thrusts: first, the systems evolution of workstations, communications, and large central processing units as the next major systems trend in both industrial and large institutional computing of all kinds; second, the proliferation of special purpose systems.

Architecture and Ease of Use

Beyond systems problems, the most important computer research in the immediate future is sure to concern software, particularly as it relates to human factors—to the effective use of systems by people. We must ask fundamental questions about how machines ought to be conceived in the first instance, so that they will be easier to use.

Today our knowledge of ergonomics is reasonably good. We understand the anthropometrics and the perceptual aspects of the relationship between hardware and human beings. A body of knowledge also exists concerning such software issues as the structure of command languages, menus, and error messages. But these are only the surface aspects of the user interface.

Clearly, the architecture of a system can have a profound influence on the quality of its human factors, yet next to nothing is known about how to make architectural decisions in the interest of human comfort. As we strive to make information systems easier to use by people who are not computer specialists, it will be increasingly important for every system architect and programmer to appreciate human factors and their effect on design. Most current computer science and engineering curricula fail in this respect. Rarely, for example, do such curricula explicitly require courses on human factors or basic psychololgy. A person can earn a Ph.D. in computer science, in anticipation of a career building tools for human beings to use, by spending many years learning how *computers* work and none learning how *human beings* work.

No wonder many users sometimes feel like the unknown computer science major at the University of Wisconsin who posted this sign above a printer in the computer center there:

> *I'm sick and tired of this machine;*
> *I wish that they would sell it.*
> *It never does just what I want,*
> *But only what I tell it.*

Revolution in Materials and Processes

Another source of university-industry interdependence comes from a revolution in materials and process engineering. Increasingly, the most useful technologies and the most productive industrial operations involve materials and processes that derive from new discoveries in science.

The high-technology challenge involves more than the chips that everyone associates with our industry. It includes the manufacturing and software engineering to create them, the systems application technology to use them, and supporting these the broad base of research in materials, magnetics, and mathematics, as well as in the computer, behavioral, and cognitive sciences.

The challenges in materials science and engineering to package and cool VLSI (very large scale integrated circuit) silicon chips, for example, are at least as great as those in the semiconductor physics behind the fabrication of the chips themselves. As we keep pushing our technology beyond conventional practice in the quest for lower costs and higher performance, we find ourselves using materials in ways never tried before in industrial applications. Indeed, even as we strive to use them in our plants some of these materials and processes exhibit properties not yet understood by science.

Thus, the dependence of industrial technology on leading-edge science grows increasingly acute. By the same token, modern science owes an increasing debt to the latest in technology, which provides the tools needed by an ever-more-sophisticated science. That's why universities are dependent upon access to industry—its labs, processes, and people—in order to contribute to advanced technologies such as microelectronics, magnetics, systems architecture, programming, and, in other fields, recombinant DNA, petroleum science, and so on.

Growing University-Industry Interaction

The interaction between high-technology companies and universities is increasing dramatically as a result of these natural and growing interdependencies. There is a new vitality in these relationships. Indeed, they are moving so fast that none of the studies on the subject—including the one done by the National Science Board last year—has anything like up-to-date figures.

IBM's University Relations Programs

As IBM has recognized exposures and dependencies, we have turned to the academic community, offering grant and contract support to encourage the development of educational plans and research in the needed areas.

Last year, for example, feeling that the training of engineers for careers in high-technology production and design for manufacturability had long been neglected, we announced a competition; we offered both computer-aided design and manufacturing equipment and grants to universities interested in developing their own curricula and their research in manufacturing systems and engineering. To our astonishment, 172 universities responded. Overall, we manage our relationships with universities to address IBM needs, which are mirrored in the economy as a whole. We make no apology for the fact that these programs are very much in IBM's own interest. Indeed, most universities prefer that our self-interest be manifest, because that frankness provides the strongest basis for lasting relationships.

Today, IBM university programs focus on working with the faculty and students, as well as responding to proposals from presidents and chancellors. The number of fellowships offered to the top departments in fields of interest to us has grown from 100 in 1981 to 221 in 1984. These fellowships are an important source of bright potential employees at the doctoral level.

We have initiated a new program of $60,000, two-year Faculty Development Awards to help untenured faculty members establish their research careers. The goal of this program is to enable universities to retain their brightest young faculty, encouraging students to complete their doctorates and contemplate an academic career.

To encourage faculty initiatives and fight red tape, 60 annual grants of $25,000 are made to top departments selected by our Research Division and laboratories. What's different about this program is that universities are not asked—or even permitted—to apply. The money can be used for anything the department likes, so long as it is "new" science or engineering.

We have over 70 IBMers on faculty loan and technical sabbaticals at colleges and universities.

The most exciting part of this story is that our cooperative research with universities has grown rapidly in recent years. More than 430 projects have been initiated, over 380 of which are currently active with 160 universities, worldwide.

Cooperative University-Industry Research

In a typical collaboration, both IBM and the university provide people. IBM provides funding and sometimes needed equipment. Money plus people plus equipment, we believe, can be far more effective than money alone. The direct contact, mutual stimulation, and professional relationships that result can be as important as what is learned.

Am I advocating turning universities into computer development laboratories? Far from it, for that is the path to the destruction of science and the frustration of industry.

Indeed, the responsibility must be placed squarely on industry to acquire the right people and set them up in the kinds of laboratories that allow them access to what's going on in our universities.

Universities As a Source of People

Universities are invaluable to industry as a source of new knowledge, but the strongest ties between us result from the universities' role as the source of industry's future employees.

Indeed, industry's share of new business and science/engineering graduates has increased 60% in the last decade. IBM hired over 5,000 college graduates and higher-degreed students in 1982 and over 3,000 so far this year. Ph.D.'s in computer science today have a training far superior to what was offered ten years ago; and it is gratifying to us that last year, for those entering industry, IBM proved the most desired employer.

Universities are motivated to promote industrial demand for their Ph.D. output, for the size of their graduate student population determines their capacity for doing research. Yet certain limitations of the university leave a major gap unfilled, for when discoveries in basic science at the university trigger whole new industries, the resulting technology moves ahead more rapidly than academic research and curriculum development can follow.

Learning By Apprenticeship

In 1963, for example, just before the announcement of System/360, IBM had thousands of people working as "computer scientists"; yet the first advanced degree in computer science was not awarded until that year. All those "computer scientists" had originally been trained as mathematicians, physicists, or engineers. They learned their computer science by apprenticeship.

Then, in the late 1960s and early 1970s, IBM became highly dependent on integrated microelectronics technology. We were early pioneers in that field, but our integrated circuit technologists were by training solid-state physicists, metallurgists, and others. They learned integrated circuit technology by apprenticeship, for no degrees in large-scale integrated electronics were granted until the late 1970s.

The same thing is true today in magnetic recording technology—an area whose revenues are so great that the number of disk media companies in the Santa Clara Valley of California alone would justify referring to it, not as Silicon Valley, but as Iron Oxide Valley. The lack of advanced university training in CAD/CAM and other advanced areas is likewise apparent.

Now, an apprentice to an old master bootmaker can learn how to make the best pair of boots in the world. But if an unexpected glitch occurs in his bootmaking, the apprentice has no base of fundamental scientific knowledge to fall back on. Basing technology on apprentice education involves a risk no technologically competitive company can afford to take—especially if it wants to be the industry leader. Industry simply must help the universities modernize their capability in order to assure our own future competitiveness.

Industry must therefore invest in the roots of the educational enterprise. The forces driving industry and academe to work together are not fabricated by some strategist, either on the fund-raising side of the university or on the public relations and marketing side of the company. They are as natural and inherent as those that cause science to spawn technology.

The fundamental driver is not research done in educational institutions but education in a forefront research environment. Because education is rooted in good research, it becomes essential for companies to get that research base in place, on the applied side as well as on the pure science side of education.

Companies that really understand what it takes to be competitive make such moves because they contribute fundamentally to long-term competitiveness, through people. We understand that our future is fundamentally linked to the universities' ability to catch up on the technological side, while continuing to lead on the scientific side. We must help universities to catch up because they cannot do so alone.

Because today's science is so dependent on the access to technology, no university can be a leader in science if it lags technologically. Neither can technological education happen unless universities can speed up, technologically.

That is why, in our own enlightened self-interest, we will collaborate ever more closely with universities to provide such help as we can, share our most challenging problems, and provide faculty and students with insight into exciting careers in our company and other technical endeavors.

And that is why the record of IBM's collaboration over many decades with Columbia University, which set its own unique pattern in the early days, is such a good precedent for the current trend and such a source of pride and satisfaction to all of us.

8. Technology in the Coming Century

ARNO PENZIAS

8. Technology in the Coming Century

ARNO PENZIAS

Ever-larger numbers of computers with ever-greater computing power, coupled with the conquest of distance by new electronic and photonic means, promise to bring enhanced capabilities for solving large-scale human problems as well as computer aided sources of enrichment of individual human lives. How well we exploit these possibilities will depend on how well we learn to think deeply and clearly about what we want information technology to do for us.

JUST AS COAL AND STEEL formed the fabric of the 19th century, the key element of the 20th has been petroleum. As we look into the future, however, it seems clear that the oil-based world economy will be superseded by a new world economy based upon information. Thus, as we preview the economy of the next century, we must focus upon the key technological advances which have brought us to what can best be described as the dawn of the Information Age.

Dramatic advances are taking place in both data processing and communications capabilities. The advent and proliferation of microprocessors bring nothing less than an explosion in computer power. At the same time, the deployment of fiber-based lightwave and sophisticated mobile radio systems promises to make the impediments of distance and movement all but irrelevant in future communications. The task of exploiting these capabilities to provide useful services presents unique challenges and opportunities. Indeed, the creation and use of software promise to become the key activities by which the economic success of advanced societies will be determined in the future. The plan of this discussion is to review each of the above areas individually, concluding with some illustrative examples of what can be synthesized from them.

Data Processing

There are computers all around us, and their numbers and power are increasing. We hear a lot about supercomputers especially. But while their power continues to increase as technology advances, the *rate* of increase has slowed considerably in recent years. Today, the interval between models with, say, twice the power of their predecessors is usually several years. Thus, unless we are able to exploit some radically new technology, our best hope for dramatic increases in supercomputer power lies in learning how to harness two or more of these machines into an efficient multi-processor configuration.

On the other hand, microprocessors have advanced from 8- to 16- to 32-bit machines, with each new device much more powerful than its predecessor. The WE™ 32100 microprocessor, for example, probably the most powerful of today's 32-bit devices, will do nearly everything that a mainframe computer will do. Using a 16-bit word you can only handle some 66,000 memory addresses at one time ($2^{16} =$ 65,836). Using 32-bit words, the number increases to more than four billion. This capacity is especially important in the support of graphic displays when each resolution element on the screen requires a separately addressable location in the computer's memory. For high-quality graphics, the number of such elements can be as large as several million, clearly more than a 16-bit machine can handle at any one time.

Figure 1.   CRAY-1 Supercomputer at AT&T Bell Laboratories

Figure 2.   WE™ 32000 Microprocessor shown in relation to a postage stamp. (This is the first 32 bit microprocessor ever put into production.)

Microprocessors are not yet as fast as large mainframe computers, but their slower speed is offset by the rapidly increasing numbers of the devices in use. The rate of world microprocessor production has already exceeded the world's human birthrate. Today, when every new automobile or appliance has one or more such devices in it, we need new standards of comparison. My favorite one is guessing the year, not too far off, when the number of microprocessors produced will exceed the number of hamburgers served by a well-known fast-food chain.

What can the processing power of all these microprocessors accomplish? To illustrate, consider what might be done with a billion (10^9) computer instructions. In the days before electronic calculators, a billion instructions was enough to do one night's math homework for all the elementary and high school children in the entire United States. If we wished to perform all the arithmetical operations for each

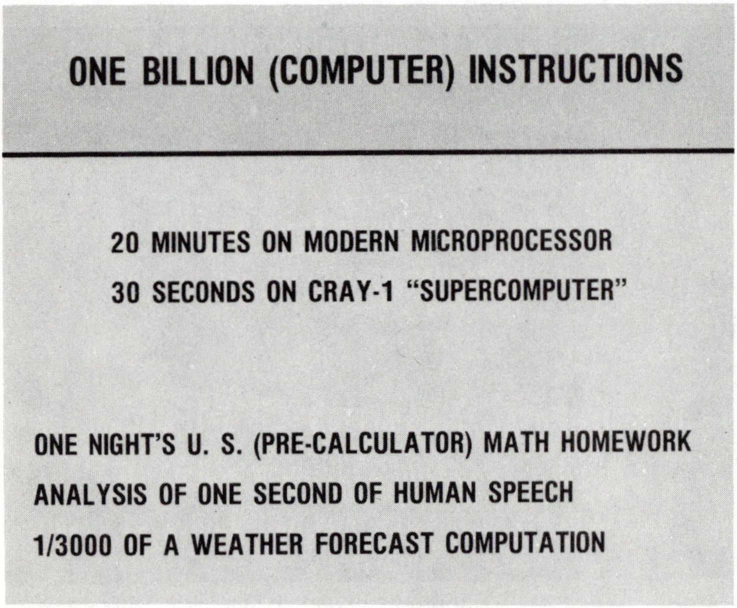

ONE BILLION (COMPUTER) INSTRUCTIONS

20 MINUTES ON MODERN MICROPROCESSOR

30 SECONDS ON CRAY-1 "SUPERCOMPUTER"

ONE NIGHT'S U. S. (PRE-CALCULATOR) MATH HOMEWORK

ANALYSIS OF ONE SECOND OF HUMAN SPEECH

1/3000 OF A WEATHER FORECAST COMPUTATION

Figure 3. One Billion Computer Instructions

student by computer, and we had the largest commercial supercomputer now available, the job would take 30 seconds. On the other hand, a present-day 32-bit microprocessor would require 20 minutes. Interestingly, the difference in power between the two is only a factor of 40. While the supercomputer is about 40 times as powerful, it costs about 40,000 times as much. Obviously, we must try to link the smaller machines together.

The need for powerful multi-microprocessor computers becomes more apparent when we consider another, more power-hungry use for a billion computer instructions. That number of instructions would be required for a computer to recognize one second's worth of speaker-independent, connected human speech. In other words, what a single stenographer does in converting spoken utterances into written text would take one billion computer instructions per second—the output of 30 supercomputers working in perfect synchronism. Since there are only a few dozen supercomputers in existence, it is not an exaggeration to note that it would take most of the world's supply of supercomputers just to replace a single stenographer. While devoting all those machines to such a task is clearly out of the question, the same task could also be done by a thousand or so microprocessors properly linked together. Furthermore, if the microprocessors were specially designed for the task, the number required ought to be at least an order of magnitude lower.

Much has been accomplished already, but we have yet to feel the full impact of the microprocessor explosion. By the end of this decade, it is likely that the computer power of a present-day supercomputer will be available in a microprocessor-based device small enough to put in one's pocket. This bold statement is all the more striking because it is based not on a consideration of the more exotic alternatives now being explored but on a simple extension of today's silicon technology. We should be looking to microprocessors to fulfill the future's immense opportunities for properly applied computing power.

Communications

The advent of lightwave communications gives us the capability of connecting widely separated data sources and processors with an ease that makes the physical distance between them all but irrelevant. Today, the United States, Japan, and much of Western Europe are being threaded with glass fiber, both to tie their major cities together and to provide a growing number of communications functions over shorter distances. Probably the most dramatic use of lightwave technology is a system now under construction which will soon span the Atlantic Ocean.

Progress has been rapid, and worldwide competition is keen. Lightwave scientists and engineers compete with one another for the high-speed lightwave distance record. The record is now held by a group of AT&T Bell Laboratories scientists who successfully transmitted a lightwave signal carrying over 400 million bits of information per second through a length of glass-fiber lightguide two hundred kilometers long, without amplification of any kind. Over somewhat shorter distances, this same group has transmitted data in excess of one billion bits per second. This means the glass fibers are so transparent that light signals generated in

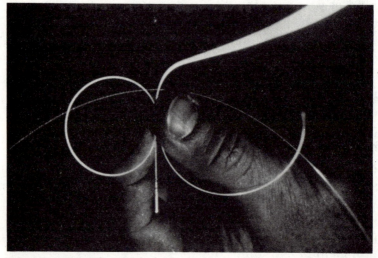

Figure 4.   Glass Fiber Lightguide

New York, for example, can be "seen" in Philadelphia.

Moreover, a single fiber can carry several billion-bit information channels, if the laser light sources are each of slightly different wavelengths, or colors. Furthermore, a modern lightwave system cable about one centimeter in diameter can have up to 144 individual fibers within it. When one multiplies the number of fibers in a cable by the number of possible "colors," one quickly sees how enormous is the potential carrying capacity of lightwave systems.

What can be supported by a transmission system operating at one billion bits per second? Three hundred two-way video conferencing signals, for example; or more than 10,000 two-way voice conversations; or three million home-computer-to-home-computer communications links of the kind most in use today (about one for every household in the city of New York). While not everyone will want a personal computer, the need for higher data rates will expand dramatically as people make increasing use of data communications, especially as more of the data is provided in pictorial form. The use of interactive video systems will put optical systems to their ultimate test. While a considerable effort must still be expended before all the promise of lightwave systems becomes a reality, I don't think it's too early to plan for the freedom from the past restrictions of distance that lightwave offers.

On another front, communications companies in the developed countries are rapidly deploying a new kind of mobile telephone service. The cellular concept, developed by AT&T Bell Laboratories engineers, overcomes problems of limited availability that plagued earlier systems. From the customer's point of view the new mobile phone works as well as today's home and office telephones do. Mobile telephones—initially in cars, later as pocket or briefcase communications terminals—for the first time permit users to call from one *person* to another, rather than from one *place* to another as we do now—another significant increase in our ability to communicate.

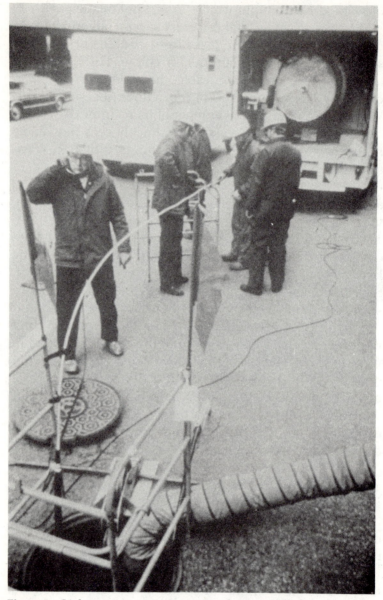

Figure 5.   Lightwave transmission system being installed

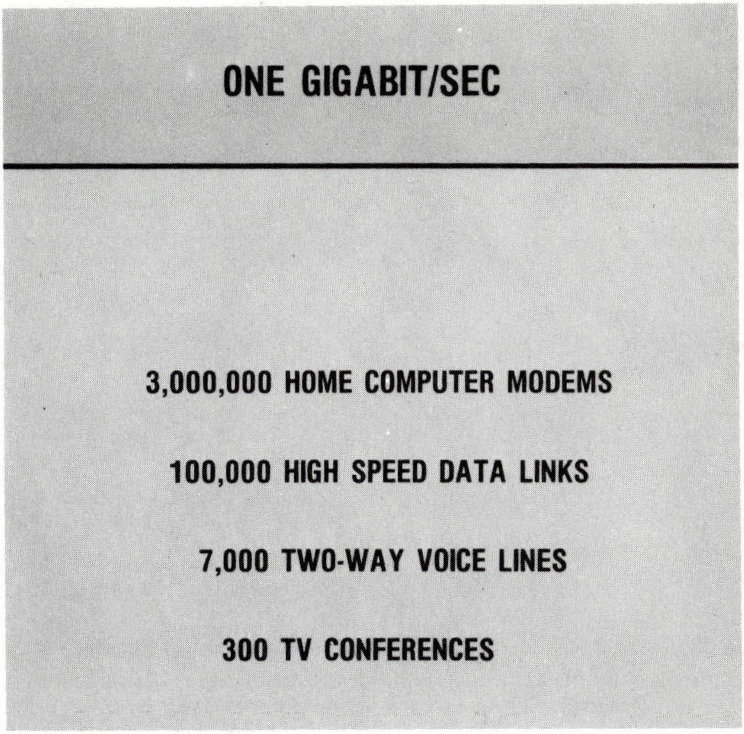

ONE GIGABIT/SEC

3,000,000 HOME COMPUTER MODEMS

100,000 HIGH SPEED DATA LINKS

7,000 TWO-WAY VOICE LINES

300 TV CONFERENCES

Figure 6. One Gigabit/Sec

Software

Software has improved much less dramatically than the power of computing and communications hardware. Despite continuing advances in computer science and programming technology, the process by which we tell our machines what we want from them is still cumbersome and tedious. Human beings usually understand one another's intentions without explicit instructions. Computers lack such understanding. Problem specification becomes more challenging with the increased complexity of the problems we ask computers to solve. Software productivity seems almost to stand still because we keep demanding more from it.

Intelligent machines may someday help us turn our ambiguously expressed wishes into formal, logically consistent statements. Efforts to program such machines are

Figure 7. Autoplex™ Mobile Communications System. (This system
extends high-quality telephone service to automobiles.)

under way in the artificial intelligence community, but progress has been difficult. The subtleties of even simple (to
human beings) narrative text are beyond all but the most
sophisticated analysis programs. For the present, useful
applications in this area appear limited to rudimentary
question-and-answer computer interfaces. The much more
difficult task of "automatic" program generation remains
unachieved.

"Expert systems," another aspect of artificial intelligence,
seems to offer more immediate payoff. By tabulating the
rules a human expert follows in confronting a problem, it is
possible to encapsulate the knowledge of humans in
machine-implementable form. Such computer programs
can give advice and provide seemingly sophisticated judg-
ments in specific, narrow fields. Expert systems are now
being used in the United States to help doctors diagnose
disease, geologists find minerals, computer manufacturers

fill complicated orders, and engineers design integrated circuits. Probably the most widely used expert system is called ACE, for Automated Cable Expertise. Developed by AT&T Bell Laboratories, it helps troubleshoot telephone lines for almost a million customers. Someday, perhaps, the knowledge of expert human programmers could be similarly mechanized and made available to help other programmers generate the software we need if we are to use computers more productively.

For the present, and probably for the foreseeable future, good software will be a commodity that should not be discarded lightly or rewritten unnecessarily. Much of the best of modern software design aims for modularity and portability so that programs can be pieced together from existing parts as needed and used on whatever computer the customer chooses.

Let me illustrate what I mean by modularity with a story that a Bell Laboratories computer scientist told me recently. Preparing a manuscript on a terminal, he became interested in word usage. Accordingly, he set out to write a text-checking program that would list the words in the manuscript in descending order of frequency. The program he wrote was surprisingly short—so short, in fact, that he decided to use it as the basis of an informal test. He began by describing the program's function to the executives of several computer companies. Their estimates of the program's length ranged between 5,000 and 20,000 lines. He next asked a number of programmers experienced in languages like Fortran and PL/1. Their answers were much lower, more like 1,000 lines of code. Programmers in the modern, more algorithmically-oriented languages like Pascal and C came up with still lower estimates, typically some 100 lines. When he asked his AT&T Bell Laboratories friends, who were familiar with the UNIX* operating system, the answers dropped to as low as a mere ten lines.

All this amused our computer scientist, for he had written the entire program in a single line of instructions that

*Trademark of AT&T Bell Laboratories.

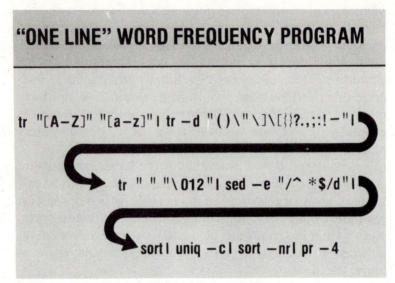

Figure 8. "One Line" UNIX Word Frequency Program

simply patched together a number of existing UNIX utilities. The reactions he got when he wrote his one-line program down on paper ranged from fascination to outrage. The latter came most often from people who considered it "cheating" not to write all their own software each time it was needed.

As for portability, the UNIX operating system runs on everything from the largest supercomputers to fingernail-sized microprocessors. Under it, programs can readily be moved from one machine to another as well as patched together as needed. The system is optimized for the convenience of the programmer instead of the machine.

While no single computer operating system or programming method is best for everyone, the advantages of portable modular building blocks over write-from-scratch systems should last at least until the time comes when software will somehow be generated effortlessly.

Opportunities for the Future

Looking toward the future, it seems reasonable to expect the use of information technology to help meet some of society's most pressing social and economic imperatives, most notably a reduction in the need for raw materials, new sources of productive employment and better lives for our people.

Of all bulk materials, petroleum's high cost and uncertain supply give it the most prominent place in the public's eye. Like those of most advanced countries, our transportation system runs on petroleum—if one may describe something that comes to an almost complete stop twice daily as "running." The perennial answer to the endless lines of creeping vehicles has been to devote yet more land, capital and materials to the construction of bigger (and "better") highways. The remarkable durability of this answer over the past half century despite evidence of its futility has provided a rich source of material for eloquent, but largely ignored, social critics. One has only to read the speeches delivered upon the occasion of the opening of the first freeway built by Los Angeles, California, hailing it as the end of the city's traffic problems.

The worldwide phenomenon of highways jamming at rush hours almost from the day they are built illustrates the simple truism that we can vitiate the use of even the most abundant resources if we handle their distribution ineptly enough. Of all resource-allocation mechanisms, congestion deserves its place as the least efficient scheme the mind of man has yet devised. Dramatically simple demonstrations of this fact abound in our personal experiences. One need only picture an impatient crowd of people attempting to push their way through a doorway to get the point.

At peak loads, stop-and-go traffic can reduce the capacity of a typical highway to a small fraction of what could be handled at normal speeds. When the airline industry was faced with a similar problem they first responded by planning more airports. By a fortunate combination of circumstances, not the least of which was that airplanes don't do well in bumper-to-bumper traffic, they were forced to a much better solution, namely scheduling. Thus, a commercial airliner is not permitted to take off until a clear flight path and landing space can be assigned to it.

While air traffic control is expensive and requires highly skilled operators, a corresponding system for highways—even including city streets and parking spaces—is conceivable as a modest add-on to an extensive network of vehicular telephones. Even today, a quite respectable 8-bit microprocessor can be bought for less than the price of a gallon of gasoline in many places. A microprocessor-based system could, among other things, automatically keep track of the location of each public bus and the number of its occupants. In an automobile it might also reserve the nearest available parking space and direct the driver to it by the least congested route.

Describing such schemes is not the same as advocating them. People may well prefer to take their chances fighting traffic rather than relinquish the "right" to schedule their trip without help. All the technologist can do is acquaint society with the range of available options, as I have attempted to do in the above example. Other examples of substituting information for raw materials include enhanced product efficiency through computer-aided design; better process control and waste avoidance in manufacturing; and longer product life through built-in maintenance, trouble-diagnosis, and repair information systems.

Let us consider next the relationships between information technology and productive employment. So much thought and discussion have been devoted to the job-producing effect of "high-tech" industry that there seems little point in adding to it here. Instead, I prefer to touch upon that portion of the labor force, very likely the large majority, who will not find what we would normally classify as high-tech work.

As our contemporary experiences with pollution, poor design, and inadequate transportation systems suggest, the present state of interaction between technology and people is not altogether positive. Moreover, when it comes to the workplace, many of us are apprehensive about technology just because it promises to work too efficiently, i.e. displace human labor. We keep hearing about "technology victims," and people being "replaced" by computers. We are confronted with the fear that the next century will be the century of the computer-replaced human being. The tale of the antagonism between man and the machine has been around for a very long time. One may recall, for example, the folk ballad about John Henry, the pile driving man, who tried to hammer an iron rod into a rock faster than the new steam-driven machine. We can admire his courage but we have reason to question his judgment. Today's machine operator would not be happy to regain the "privilege" of wielding a hammer.

The basic question is whether machines will be our competitors or our servants. The latter seems the more likely choice, given the range of options technology will offer. Indeed, it seems likely that the coming century will produce not the computer-*replaced* but the computer-*enhanced* human being.

Consider a mundane example—a cab driver's business prospects. Today it seems the only way he can increase his income is by running traffic lights. Tomorrow he might be able to go into other businesses, by equipping the passenger compartment with a mobile telephone, an attached computer terminal, and a printer. (I'd also recommend an electronic credit card reader.) For a fee a tourist might buy theater tickets on the way downtown, look at a weather report on the way to the airport, review stock market quotes or the latest news from home in his own language, all on a handy display screen. As a computer-aided human being the taxi driver provides a concrete example of the potential synergy between human and technological capabilities.

Productivity also improves when one can perform work for oneself which would otherwise have gone undone. Here let us consider the mother who is homebound with a sick child. In the future she might be able to solve her problem by turning on a video display terminal and dialing a data base containing the child's pertinent characteristics.

By either touching the touch-sensitive screen or talking to the set, she would define the problem in an interactive session with an appropriate computer system. If the system diagnosed a simple cold, medicine could be prescribed and delivery arranged. In a more serious case, two-way contact with a human physician could quickly be established. Thus instead of relying on a home health-care manual, the mother could use properly designed information technologies to function as an effective medical technician.

Last, let us turn to ways in which Information Age technologies promise to enhance our abilities, and how we might use these abilities to enrich our lives. To artists, for example, computers offer a new medium in which to express themselves. Historians can uncover and examine heretofore inaccessible clues by looking at data in new ways. Scientists can ask new questions of nature. But time-wasters can also waste more time. In the final analysis, therefore, it seems that computers can only enhance whatever we already are.

This gloomy assessment overlooks the human capacity for learning, adaptation, and growth. The fate of the human species—and the impact of both nature and our inventions on our lives—depends on our ability to educate ourselves for the future.

If we seek to better educate the millions of people who have not been well served by our traditional educational system, we will need tools beyond the capabilities offered by present-day classroom computers. Truly flexible machines with natural-language understanding, speech and image recognition, access to libraries of expert systems, a full range of data base delivery systems, and much more will be needed. With the advent of such machines, an instructor with prior knowledge of the subject matter may no longer be needed. Instead, a "learning partner" role may emerge—someone to provide structure, motivation, and discipline, but having no more education than the "student." A grandparent, older sibling, friend, or fellow employee could "teach" and learn at the same time, providing the human component that even the most powerful of machines will never have.

This human sharing in the quest of knowledge may well be the brightest promise offered by the technology of the Information Age.

In order to fulfill this and the other promises, we must not only make imaginative use of existing technology, but the users of technology must also enter into a partnership of understanding with the creators and implementors of technology to guide and encourage additional progress toward mankind's common goals.

9. Computer Science: Challenges and Responsibilities

JOSEPH F. TRAUB

9. Computer Science: Challenges and Responsibilities

JOSEPH F. TRAUB

In most disciplines, building a department of national distinction would suffice. The role of computers is so central that computer scientists have responsibilities beyond the discipline and the department. There are opportunities and responsibilities for service to the institution, the city, the region, and the nation that have far-reaching social and educational implications.

ELSEWHERE in this book are essays by nine distinguished leaders of American technology. I want to use this opportunity to tell you briefly about computer science at Columbia, and to speak of our responsibilities to this university, to the Greater New York area, and to the nation.

The Computer Science Department was founded on July 1, 1979; so we've just passed our fourth birthday. That fall, Peter Likins and I submitted a proposal to the IBM Corporation entitled "Towards a Computer Science Department of Great Distinction." We asked IBM to help us realize a dream, the creation of a great computer science department at Columbia.

Specifically, we requested funds for the first stage in the development of the new department. The first stage was to take five years, and we listed eight objectives to be accomplished in that time. The eight objectives listed in that proposal were to:

1. Attract a faculty of national caliber.

2. Attract a student body of national caliber.

3. Acquire first-rate experimental facilities.

4. Acquire suitable space to house the computer science department.

5. Gain national and local recognition as a focus for research and education in computer science.

6. Secure substantial funding from federal and corporate sources.

7. Develop cooperation with appropriate departments and schools of Columbia university.

8. Develop cooperation with corporations both nationally and in the Greater New York Area.

That five year plan was submitted in October, 1979.

I have resisted the temptation to tell you what we have accomplished with respect to each of these objectives. Statistics about offspring tend to be more interesting to parents than to listeners. I want only to tell you that we've met each of the eight objectives either fully or in large measure, and I'd like to briefly summarize the highlights.

Our first objective was to attract a faculty of national caliber. At a time when the national media have been reporting the difficulty of attracting any good computer science faculty, we have attracted a superb group. Each year we get some 150 applications and we have hired the cream. Our faculty is at the frontiers of the most challenging areas: we're designing and building supercomputers; designing VLSI chips; working on computer networking and distributed computing; studying algorithms and complexity; and working on languages and operating systems. We have great strength in artificial intelligence, where we do research on vision, natural language understanding, expert systems, and learning.

It is the faculty which has made everything else possible. There are some 400 majors, including 60 carefully selected Ph.D. students, and 4000 students are enrolled in our courses, including students from all four of Columbia's undergraduate colleges, the graduate school and a number of the professional schools. With the help of a major equipment gift from DEC we have constructed an outstanding research facility. In just four years we raised our research funding to some four million dollars a year. Those monies come from both the federal government and the private sector. Columbia has been designated as a New York State Center for Computers and Information Systems; the Computer Science Department will play a major role as part of that Center.

We've also developed mutually beneficial relations with many parts of the university and with both local and national corporations.

Finally, we recently moved into a beautiful building which provided the excuse to get together with our friends on this occasion.

Those are some of the accomplishments of the last four years. They would have been impossible without the wholehearted and vigorous support of Columbia's administration and its Board of Trustees.

We've done very well, but we are not yet in the very top tier of the nation's computer science departments. Since the objectives of our first five-year plan were realized a year early, the time is ripe to plan the next step. My colleagues and I are currently doing just that.

In most disciplines, building a department of national distinction would suffice. But I believe the role of computers is so central that we have responsibilities beyond building the discipline and the department.

We have a responsibility to this great university. Up to now, the impact of computers has been felt most strongly in disciplines where quantification and calculation are important. Examples are the sciences, business, engineering, the social sciences, and medicine. Next will be fields where the collection and dissemination of information are central, and thus we are starting to see the transformation of the libraries, and journalism. The graphical capabilities of computers are starting to change architecture.

But I believe some of the most startling changes will occur in the arts and humanities. In some ways, the impact there is predictable (word processing, electronic mail, new media for artists) but the predictable part is the least interesting. The truly revolutionary changes are not predictable, just as five hundred years ago, our forebears could not have forseen such consequences of Gutenberg's invention as the Reformation, the rise of nationalism, and the astonishing growth of science.

By computers I don't mean machines that manipulate numbers, although they do that very well indeed. When I refer to computers, I mean new media, new forms of communication, new ways to create and gain access to information, new methods of teaching and learning, and new paradigms for understanding the human mind.

I have devoted entire talks to discussing why computers will transform universities—I don't mean the comptroller's and the registrar's offices, but the intellectual heart of the university. Here, I will limit myself to stating my belief that in the future the comparative excellence of major universities may relate directly to their comparative excellence in the use of computers.

I must emphasize that we are not trying to change Columbia into a university of computer scientists, although we would like to attract some of the best and brightest. It is exactly the diversity and richness of a great university that attracted many computer scientists to Columbia. Our job is to enrich, not to homogenize. What we must do is make the best and most appropriate information processing available to the diverse elements that make up Columbia

In addition to our responsibility to Columbia, we have an obligation to the Greater New York area. This region has extraordinary strengths. It is the financial, corporate, and media center of the country, and therefore the world. It is home to several of the world's leading research laboratories, and to many fine high-technology companies. It may have the highest density of computers in the world.

New York has long been a great commercial center. But the nature of commerce and of business has changed. The great ports, rivers, and canals are now electronic. In high technology we are not viewed as a national leader. That distinction belongs to California and Massachusetts. Texas is now mobilizing for a serious challenge. Other parts of the country are developing ambitious plans. This region must decide on its goals and how it is to go about achieving them. New York State has made a start through the New York State Science and Technology Foundation, and as I mentioned earlier, Columbia University has been designated as the New York State Center for Advanced Technology in Computers and Information Systems.

That is only a start. We must decide, possibly as a region, or as individual states, whether we wish to play a national leadership role in high technology. If the answer is yes, we must decide how we go about achieving that goal.

Finally, there are issues which transcend university and region. You can hardly read a newspaper, news magazine, or business journal without reading about them. There are many such issues and I will mention only a few. The United States domination in computers has lasted so long that some may deem it preordained—our manifest destiny. I assure you it is not preordained; other nations are making serious challenges. If we lose our preeminence, the economic and national security consequences will be severe. The reason is simple. Computing is the technology that drives all other technologies.

I'll list some additional national issues: privacy; computer crime; the appalling state of our education system; shifts in employment due to automation; and the widening gap between the information haves and have-nots, both in the United States and between the developed and Third World nations. Finally, because the decision times have become so brief, there is the danger that computers will make decisions of war and peace.

On most of these issues, the Computer Science Department will not be taking stands as a department. But some of us are playing active roles as individuals. For example, a number of us at Columbia are engaged in alerting both ordinary citizens and our government to the serious challenges now posed by other nations to our dominance in computing.

Many of the national issues I've listed are political, and what the department must do is help to ensure that we have an educated citizenry that understands what living with computers means and thus can participate intelligently in discussions and policy decisions that concern these issues.

The convocation will reach its climax when Columbia confers the Doctor of Science, *honoris causa*, on Professor Herbert A. Simon. Herb, I and many others have learned so much from you. I look forward to the award ceremony with special anticipation.

10. Cohabiting the Planet with Computers

HERBERT A. SIMON

(Left to Right) JOSEPH F. TRAUB, Chairman, Computer Science Department, Columbia University, HERBERT A. SIMON, MICHAEL I. SOVERN, President, Columbia University.

CITATION

HERBERT A. SIMON
For the Degree of Doctor of Science

A profound and original scientist, you have pursued answers to a great and even glorious question: how do we think? In that pursuit, you have made outstanding contributions to a dazzling variety of fields, including political science, sociology, philosophy, computer science, psychology and economics. So distinguished are your contributions that your colleagues have seen fit to confer upon you their highest honors in three distinct fields, including the Nobel Memorial Prize in economics.

You have introduced the concept of bounded rationality—that humans are only human, living in a complex world which they must drastically simplify in order to make decisions; you pioneered in the introduction of the computer as a laboratory instrument for modeling human cognitive processes; you have insisted on systematic observation and experimentation to discover the fundamental laws in the social sciences. Your quest for the simple hidden within the complex aims toward the larger explanation—the sciences—of the artificial, or artifacts of the mind.

For a career devoted to the pursuit of knowledge that has enhanced both the understanding of what we know, and also how we know it, Columbia University is honored to confer upon you the degree of Doctor of Science, *honoris causa*.

Michael I. Sovern
President

October 11, 1983

10. Cohabiting the Planet with Computers

HERBERT A. SIMON

How different will the future seem to us when we are surrounded by billions of computers, as we soon will be? Dr. Simon shows that we have been living in the midst of computers for a very long time, and draws on our experience with them to assess the possible contributions of the new electronic computers to an improvement in the human condition.

FROM OTHER SPEAKERS we have heard something of the early history of computing at Columbia, which stretches all the way back to the Watson Lab here in the 1920s. When, as a graduate student at another university, I first became enamored of punched cards as a relief from statistical drudgery, the Watson Lab was prominent in the development of scientific applications of that technology. So what we have here is certainly not the birth, but a new efflorescence of the important field of computer science at Columbia University.

We are not only celebrating new developments at this institution, but more broadly and widely we are celebrating the excitement of computer science as a domain of intellectual inquiry. At any given point in history a few areas of science—not a long list of them—especially attract bright young people by their promise of intellectual adventure.

Two characteristics of a field of knowledge make it an especially exciting area in which to do science. First, it should address a fundamental human question, a question that concerns people—even bothers people—at a deep level. And second, in order to be exciting science the field must have a method or methods for tackling that question. You can have all the profound questions you like, but unless there is something you can do about them, unless there is a first step of inquiry that you can take, those are not exciting scientific questions; they're just enigmatic human puzzles.

What are the good questions and methods today, the questions and methods that are attracting the brightest graduate students? Four domains of science clearly head my own list of exciting fields. When I tell you what they are, you will probably find that I have omitted your favorite. You can add it as a fifth.

One scientific question that has been on the list a long time is the nature of matter. We've had an exciting adventure, indeed, in this century exploring the nature of the fundamental particles that make up the material world. In the past half century, the principal tools for the inquiry have been the great machines that we call particle accelerators. They have enabled us to probe into the nature of matter at more and more profound and esoteric levels.

The second scientific question on my list, closely related to the first, is the nature of the universe—the cosmological question, you might say. And here again, we've been able to peer deeper and deeper into space—perhaps even *around* space—because we have developed powerful methods and instruments for doing so: radio telescopes, space probes, and the mathematical tools that go along with them and enable us to interpret what they see.

The third question on my list is the nature of life. We have long had a deep curiosity about living things and what distinguishes them from the nonliving—or today I suppose we should say, how living things can emerge from the nonliving. And here again a whole range of powerful tools have evolved for searching out the answers to these questions, from the electron microscope and radioactive tracers to recombinant DNA.

The fourth question on my list is the nature of mind, including the celebrated mind-body problem. For centuries, even millennia, that question has been on the philosopher's agenda, but without adequate tools for tackling it. For lack of a means of approach, it would have been hard to place it on the list of exciting scientific questions until quite recently. But in the past thirty years we have acquired the tools we need, most notably the digital computer, for asking ourselves (and for getting at least partial answers to) the question "What is Mind?" That question now belongs on the short list of good research problems; and the field of computer science, which attempts to solve the problem, may be added to the list of domains where exciting science can be done.

Computers and the Nature of Mind

What do computers have to do with the nature of mind? Today, perhaps, the answer is pretty widely known, and I needn't say much about it; although as recently as five years ago I might have felt obliged to devote my entire talk to it. Briefly, the computer can reveal the nature of mind because the human mind is a computer, and because some computers (at least, some computers programmed in some ways) are minds, or even collections of minds. That the mind is a computer and that computers are minds is a hypothesis that Allen Newell and I have called the "Symbol System Hypothesis." Of course it is an empirical hypothesis. It may seem implausible to you or it may seem self-evident to you; but the proper way to test it is by the usual methods of science, to confront it with facts. We can test it by studying minds, by studying computers, and by seeing what the relation is between them. In particular, we can test it by seeing how it is that both human minds and computers can think.

I don't want to review the evidence for the Symbol System Hypothesis here. I'm going to ask you—those of you who haven't already reviewed it and who don't already accept it—to make, for the moment, a great leap of faith. I'm going to ask you to accept it as a hypothesis so that we may inquire into its consequences, if true. Let us see where the hypothesis leads, and especially where it leads with respect to the position of the human species, our species, in a world full of computers. (The world is also full of people. Sometimes we think it's a little too full of people, but that's another set of questions that I can't address here.)

How are we going to cohabit this planet of ours, not only with the other 3,999,999,999 or so human beings, but also with the billions, perhaps tens of billions, of computers that will also be here?

As I listen to public discussion about computers, and particularly discussion about computers as intelligent systems, systems that think, I hear many expressions of uneasiness. There seems to be special uneasiness about cohabiting a world with computers when some of them might turn out to be smarter than we humans are. Partly, of course, the discomfort with computers is the kind of unease we feel in dealing with anything new and strange. Until we have had a chance to assess it, each new thing comes into the world as kind of a Rorschach inkblot. We look at that blot of ink and read into it all of our hopes or, more often, all of our anxieties. And whether we form an optimistic view of what it means for us or a pessimistic view probably depends much less on the shape of the inkblot than it does on the balance in our own psyche between hopes and anxieties.

We might feel better and more relaxed about living in the world with computers if we recognized that in most ways it is not a new world. In saying that, I suppose I am aligning myself with the forces of reaction, for we have certainly heard a great deal about the novelties and innovations that computers will introduce into our future. Without disagreeing in the least with such predictions, however, I wish to propose that, in fundamental ways, this future is not going to seem very different to us from the present or the recent past. I will argue that we are already thoroughly familiar with computers and that mankind has long been familiar with them; that the novelty the new electronic computers bring us is largely a novelty of understanding what mind is, not a novelty that requires us to understand and live in a new kind of world.

As evidence for my reactionary proposal, I'm going to present a few examples of computers that we have lived with for a long time—since long before we'd invented electronics. Reminding you of them may suggest ways of thinking about the computer you've just purchased at your neighborhood store and adopted into your home. In particular, these venerable examples will give us insight into a world in which we not only have personal computers, but in which all of these computers are interconnected in networks.

We have had a good deal of discussion in this gathering not only about the little computers you can have on your desks, but also about the linkage of those computers through the whole office, the whole company, or for that matter, the whole world. We have even had it proposed to link these computers to New York's taxicabs, with unpredictable effects on the kinds of conversations we will have with their drivers. The computers that my examples refer to are precisely these kinds of interconnected networks.

Examples of Familiar Computers: Physical Systems

I shall propose four examples of networked computers. Unless you are a pantheist, you will find it hard to think of the first two as minds, but they certainly are computers. The third and fourth examples are computers that also are definitely minds. As you may have guessed by now, my first example is the solar system.

The solar system is a very large computer that makes innumerable computations in the shortest periods of time. In fact, it is a continuous computer that can only be represented mathematically by differential equations—difference equations won't do the trick. Obviously it is a distributed system, with computations going on simultaneously in all of its components, each responding to the presence and location of the others.

The solar system is a computer that has the utmost effect

on our lives. It determines the climate we live in, determines when we get up in the morning and when we go to bed at night. I restrict myself to its natural effects, known by the methods of science, and leave out of my account the astrological inferences that some people draw from this computer, or its possible influence on the business cycle.

The solar system is the kind of computer that we call a physical system. That is to say, it is self-referential; it doesn't make computations about other systems. What it computes is its own behavior. It is, so to speak, its own orrery, although we human beings sometimes find pleasure in building miniature orreries of it.

Thus, the solar system is not a symbolic computer, as some of the computers are that I will talk about later. Those computers, we shall see, refer to something other than themselves; are able to talk not simply to themselves and about themselves, but also about other things. But the solar system is interesting in the present world of computers because its computations are highly distributed. It is a parallel computer, each planetary body (really each molecule or atom in the planetary bodies) being a component.

Gordon Bell has spoken of the difficulty of building parallel computers with large numbers of components. Nature has no such difficulty. In the solar computer each component does its own thing, a phenomenon you can interpret in two ways. By one interpretation, each component accelerates in response to the components around it. By the other interpretation, each component exerts forces on all the components around it, influencing their behavior. You can therefore think of the solar system either as one in which each particle is dominated by the system as a whole, with no freedom of its own, or as a system in which each particle is active, telling all the other particles something of what they should be doing. I myself prefer the second, the force-exerting or (so to speak) free-will interpretation of the solar system.

We learn at least two important lessons from this example. We learn, first of all, how order can emerge from highly decentralized but interrelated forces—how we can

have design without a Designer. There's no central con-
troller who says, "Mars, you go there . . . Sun, you step over
there." It's not arranged like the ceremony at a convocation.
Each of the bodies knows exactly where it should go
without this kind of central direction.

From the example we learn, second, how through two billion years of adaptation (if that's the right number) the very
terms of our own existence, of the human condition, were
defined by the computations of this system. For example,
the energy-rich chemical bonds that allow living things to
use energy from the sun are adapted to just the range of
energy levels that impinge on them near Earth's surface. If
the solar system had evolved with quite a different distance
between Earth and Sun, the organic molecules on which
present life depends would be inert or would dissociate. So
the orrery we call the solar system defines the limits of our
freedom as human beings.

There are no gravity shields; all of us must obey the law of
gravitation, and all the other natural laws as well. But
within the limits of those laws, we, as components of the
system, can and must make all sorts of decisions and
choices. The system combines regulation with a wide range
of autonomy for components.

My second example of a physical computer system,
closely dependent on the first, is the atmosphere, the
weather. It is a physical computer decentralized right down
to the level of the individual molecules. It has so many
degrees of freedom that building a meteorological orrery or
model of any kind stretches the capacities of even our
largest computers. The task of the NCAR laboratory in Colorado, which has been striving for many years to model the
atmosphere and the weather, is to find a computer big
enough to predict the weather as rapidly as the weather
happens. The task can be approximated only by settling for
an extremely crude model of the meteorological system.
Each improvement of grain size in the model—each refine-
ment of the network of coordinates—calls for an enormous
increase in computing power.

What do we learn from the atmospheric computer? We

learn that even a determinate machine—and it surely is that—can behave in ways so nearly chaotic that it almost forecloses the possibility of prediction. We can glimpse only statistical order in it. And as with the solar system, the atmospheric system has the gravest consequences for our lives. We deal with those consequences mainly not by fighting the system, but by adapting to it. We've made only minor, and I think dubiously successful, attempts to intervene in an active way in the computation by such measures as cloud seeding.

We respect and sometimes fear both of these physical computing systems—the solar and atmospheric systems—because they are smarter than we are. They can do all sorts of things that we can't comprehend. We recognize the control they exercise over our lives and our very nature, but we don't perceive them as denying our humanity. Rather, they define it. Nor do we perceive them as impinging on our freedom, for we define our freedom within obedience to natural law.

Examples of Familiar Computers: Social Systems

Let me turn to a pair of systems that may be more recognizable to you as computers than the solar or atmospheric systems were. Both are major components of a more comprehensive computer that we call society. Moreover, unlike the physical computers that we have just been considering, these computers are symbol systems. They get their work done, they operate, by creating, modifying, and exchanging symbols.

The two computers I have in mind are the political system and the economic system. Their components, at least up to the present era, have been almost exclusively human—thinking, believing, and feeling human beings. Their computations are performed by the interaction of the millions, tens of millions, or hundreds of millions of human components who inhabit a nation.

I'll mention only the most obvious ways in which the political system computes: by electing, and by legislating. The political system contributed a very important idea in the early days of electronic computing. A generation ago, hardware reliability was much more difficult to attain than it is now. To overcome the problem, von Neumann and others conceived the idea of making every computation an odd number of times and, in case of disagreement among the outcomes, accepting the majority vote. So the idea in computing of using majority logic was taken over quite directly from the computing system that we call a democratic political system.

I would not like to insist too strongly on the significance of that analogy, but certainly our political institutions have to be viewed as distributed computers operating under a regime of majority logic. Moreover, each of the components of this political computer is itself a complex subsystem.

We have no lack of experience with the computer called the political system; we're all highly familiar with it. We often rail against it in despair at the inadequacy of its performance. Its computational power does not seem to match the difficulty of the problems we pose it. Yet, in its almost inscrutable operation (for surely none of us would claim to understand at a deep level how it works), the computer we call our political system is able to maintain, most of the time, a tolerable level of order and tranquility and sometimes even some measure of justice in a large society. Political systems also experience sometimes rather spectacular computational failures, which make much of the stuff with which history books are filled. Although, the political computer exercises enormous influence over our lives, yet in the interstices of the regularities it computes and imposes, it can permit its human components an enormous amount of freedom and self-determination. It may even allow the freedom to alter and loosen the constraints themselves, to modify the connections, you might say, of the hardware and the program by which it operates.

My fourth, and closely related, example is the economic system. It is perhaps the most remarkable computer of all. For a highly idealized abstraction of the economy, ingenious economists can prove optimality theorems of great mathematical beauty. The economic system, too, is a distributed

computer that organizes a complex system with explicit recognition of individual differences in values and prefer-
ences. To mention just an instance, it determines how many
of us, among those who would like to be professional poets,
can actually earn our livings writing verse. This generaliza-
tion applies to all other occupations as well.

I don't want to deify the economic computer. We must, by
all means, avoid deifying computers; they are not the new
idol, the new Baal. One problem with the economic system
is that we understand it so poorly, though we are its components, that we are unable to fine-tune it. We seem not to
know how to attain full employment without inflation, or
stable prices without unacceptable levels of unemployment. In terms of our ability to control it, the economic computer is a blunt instrument. It gets our economic business
done at some moderate level of effectiveness and with
some, often justified, measure of grumbling. As we know, it
also has great potential for instability. As those who understand the mathematics of dynamic systems can tells us, that
instability arises especially because each component computer in the economic system can try to outguess the future
behavior of the other components. This potential for instability is magnified by the fact that each component can also
communicate with the other components and thereby syn-
chronize their attempts to outguess each other. With all of
these defects, the economic system operates tolerably a
large part of the time.

The Impact of Computers

Since we have lived a long while with these two social computers, the political system and the economic system, both
of which do genuine symbolic computation, we have a substantial basis in experience for evaluating the potential
impact of computers on our lives. We know that a distributed computing system with intelligence at each of its
nodes can organize, more or less well, the affairs of a
society. At the same time, it can allow enormous autonomy
to its components, accommodating diversity and even con-
flict of values.

Up to this point, except in my introductory remarks, I haven't said a word about what the effect might be of introducing electronic components into these computers. That is really what the computer revolution now going on is all about. As others before me have emphasized, we are entering a stage of human society when electronic computers—this new species or genus—are going to enter at every point into the existing distributive computers that we are now using to manage our affairs.

If the new electronic computers are to have major social significance, that significance will be mediated through their impact on these larger systems, the political and economic. We shouldn't expect the basic characteristics of the economic or political system to change simply because we insert multitudes of new intelligent units into them. Growth of population is no new phenomenon.

People who are sanguine about artificial intelligence suppose that many of our economic problems would go away if we had computer models that could predict business cycles and trends accurately. Models that try to do this exist already, and although they probably do somewhat better than pure guessing, no one is very happy about their predictive performance. But suppose we did have a computer that could predict the business cycle, or predict what would happen when certain governmental policies were initiated. We can estimate the effect by supposing we had a human being who could to the same thing. What would be the consequences?

Such a human being (or computer) would be a great thing. It would probably help us to manage our affairs better than we manage them today. But there's no magic solution to economic problems in the electronics of a computer. We don't predict business cycles very well, not because our computers are protoplasmic rather than electronic, but because we don't have good models of the economic phenomena themselves. The question is one of knowledge and intelligence, regardless whether in human or electronic brains.

So the new electronic computers recruited and brought

into the social system by its present human members—
elected to the club, as it were—will augment the intelligence
of the present participants in the system, and will augment
it while pursuing the goals of those participants. What does
this imply? If you believe that social life, the game of society,
is a zero-sum game, in which someone must lose when
another gains, then you will be greatly concerned about
how this new intelligence is distributed among the players;
for the introduction of all of these new computers might tilt
the balance and considerably influence who are going to be
the winners and who the losers. Introduction of this new
component in the system will concern you as would any
other shift in the distribution of political power in the body
politic.

To the extent, however, that social life is not a zero-sum
game, so that, in the words of Alice, "All will be winners; all
shall have a prize," the total product of the system can be
increased by introduction of the new computers. These new
players can be expected to add substantially, through their
intelligences, to our ability to meet basic human needs and
provide things that human beings value. Far from threatening our humanity or welfare, computers can contribute
greatly to both. They can supply a large portion of new intelligence with which to address social and environmental
problems. And in particular, their new intelligence can be
applied to improve the political and economic computing
systems.

What I must emphasize again is that the consequences of
introducing new sources of intelligence into these systems
will have nothing to do with whether the intelligence is
electronic or not. Rather, the consequences will hinge on
the quality of the intelligence supplied.

Let me return for a moment to the primordial fear I mentioned earlier, of creatures that are smarter than we are. Will
the computers gang up on us? Will there be a class war, as
there was in Čapek's play *R. U. R.*, this time a struggle not
of the proletariat against the factory owners but of electronic
devices against human beings?

The notion of computers ganging up on human beings is

an excellent theme for science fiction; but why do we suppose that because we introduce a myriad of electronic components into a large distributive system those components will have a common interest, a class interest? It's much more likely that they, like us, will work toward the interests of many organizations, many social entities, small and large. Sometimes they will compete with each other, and sometimes they'll collaborate, even as you and I do. They will raise the level of intelligence of that competition and cooperation.

While we know that intelligence can be used toward all human ends, good or bad, we have some reason for believing that a deeper understanding of our problems, both the problems of dealing with nature and those of dealing with each other, can cause our competition to be less self-defeating and our cooperation to be more effective. Isaac Asimov's First Law of Robotics requires that a robot must never under any circumstances harm a human being. A weaker, but still acceptable, principle is that computers will contribute to society distributed intelligence, that intelligence will garner increases of knowledge; and that, on the average and in the long run, knowledge is always better than ignorance.

Scientists doing basic research would face a deep moral dilemma if we didn't believe that proposition: that, on the average and in the long run, knowledge is better than ignorance. For when we work in basic science, we cannot presume to know the eventual uses of our discoveries. Unless a look back over human history encourages us to lay a general bet that it is better for human beings to know than to remain ignorant, we lack a moral basis for our scientific work and cannot legitimately ask that social resources be allocated to support it.

In my lifetime, the world's population has increased from fewer than two billion souls to more than four billion. Countless new intelligences have been brought into the world and have been hooked into the world's social computers. These happen to have been human intelligences, which, by the way, make heavy resource demands upon the environment. One of our problems today is that the world's resources can hardly support the bodies containing all the human intelligence that now exists.

Of course the prospective resource demands of electronic computers should also concern us, and we should begin to ask ourselves just what those requirements are. I don't think they are well known. Computers may not eat food, but they do consume a considerable amount of air conditioning, just to mention one of their needs; so the computer revolution doesn't come without resource costs.

But setting aside the issue of resource allocation, when we bring new human computers into the world, we don't consider their intelligence a threat to the others already here. Most of us do not toss on our beds at night worrying about the fact that other people are smarter than we are. If we do have that worry, we should regard it as pathological and seek professional help. On the contrary, many of us hope that the smarter people in the world can solve some of the problems that are too hard for us. Hence, if we can increase human intelligence by supplementing it with artificial intelligence, this should be cause for rejoicing.

The talks preceding mine gave us glimpses of the new world—pictures so clear that I wondered whether there would be anything left for me to talk about. In fact, these splendid visions may be what forced me into the conservative position that I'm taking now.

Since I can't discuss or even allude to all the preceding talks, let me use just one of them to help me make my next point. In his talk on the electronic university, Bob Spinrad evoked a day in the life of a student, a professor, and a dean. All of them were living in the brave new world, surrounded by—one might say immersed in—computers. What struck me about their world was how closely it resembled the one in which we already live. How like this electronic university was the university I've always known. I don't mean just the university of the past ten years, for as a computer scientist I have indeed been living immersed in computers. It's just like the university and the world in the days before the Second World War, when computers were only a gleam in a few people's eyes. Of course we didn't get our class assignments by computer mail, and didn't learn about the evening's concert from the computer bulletin board. We had to go to a bulletin board of cork and lath and read words printed on paper. But how superficial those differences are in relation to the familiarity of the human needs, desires, and values expressed in the story of the electronic university. The young man in the story enjoyed concerts. He could be trapped into a certain amount of excitement and interest in his intellectual work if the assignments of his professor were clever enough. He had a girlfriend. So what's new in this world? It would be perfectly understandable to anyone who inhabited a pre-computer campus.

If we take an even longer perspective, say of 2,000 or even 10,000 years, we see that technological progress has profoundly altered mankind's environment, so that today it is predominantly artificial. But along certain important basic dimensions, that technological development has changed very little in ourselves. We can read the Hebrew prophets, the Greek dramatists, or the Greek philosophers and historians and with little difficulty put ourselves in their places, feel their human emotions, empathize with their existential problems. Our ability to communicate in this way with the distant past is some measure of the stability of the human species in the face of tremendous environmental and institutional change. We talk freely about technological revolutions and computer revolutions. The day when we should capitalize "Revolution," perhaps write the whole word in capitals, is the day when we can no longer understand what the plays of Euripides are about. That failure of understanding will signal a change in the human condition of the most fundamental sort.

There have been over the centuries not only technological revolutions, but innumerable social revolutions as well. In our own time, at least two of these—the Russian and the Chinese—have tried deliberately to produce a New Man, a person who would have motivations and relations to the larger social computer that differed significantly from those that govern human behavior in other societies. Most scholars who have studied and evaluated those revolutions have concluded that whatever else they have accomplished, whatever else they have changed, they have not produced the New Man. The motives and behavior of people in Moscow and Beijing today are at least as easy to understand as those of Thucydides' Athenians or the denizens of the sacred halls of Columbia University.

Conclusion

How do we add up all of this? First, we need not approach computers, even myriads of interlinked computers we will deal with in the world ahead, as novelties, incomparable to anything we already understand. As a matter of fact, we have had a very long experience with complex computing systems, and that experience allows us to go far in understanding the systems that are now emerging. Or at least it prevents us from misunderstanding them more profoundly than we misunderstand the computers we have been living with through these long ages.

Each of us today is surrounded by computers that affect our lives. The computations of the planets, the computations of the atmosphere, the political computations of all our fellow citizens and ourselves, the computations of everyone in the marketplace—these are the computations and computers we live with and are familiar with. All of these are smarter than any computers we can now manufacture and program, although this may no longer be true in the year 2000.

Let's ask about these familiar computational systems the question that is now so frequently asked about electronic computers. Do these systems control us? Yes, in certain important senses they do, for they set vital limits to our behavior and its consequences. But usually we don't think of them as controlling us; usually we view them as defining the space within which we do our own computations.

Nor is our computational space a fixed space; human intelligence has continually enlarged it over the history of our species. When human intelligence is generously augmented with machine intelligence, we will have means for enlarging again the space of our thoughts, our hopes, and our actions. As in the past, we will sometimes use those means well and sometimes badly. But we retain our hope and belief that, on balance, our new intelligence will bring some measure of improvement in the human condition. As in the past, we will prefer knowledge to ignorance.

The Authors

 WILLIAM F. MILLER is a physicist-turned-computer scientist, academic administrator, business executive, and venture capitalist. Since 1979, he has served as president and chief executive officer of SRI International, a diversified, worldwide research and consulting organization headquartered in Menlo Park, California. Born and educated in Indiana, Dr. Miller moved to Stanford University as Professor of Computer Science in 1965, following a decade of work (1955–1965) with Argonne National Laboratory, first as Associate Physicist, then as Director of the Applied Mathematics Division. His varied appointments at Stanford include the Herbert Hoover Professorship of Public and Private Management (1979–), Associate Provost for Computing (1968–1971), Vice President and Provost (1971–1978). His varied interests and talents have involved him in a number of directorships, governmental commissions (including, currently, the National Science Board), educational and scholarly offices, and have brought to him and his associates many honors and awards in a productive career that shows no signs of slowdown or lack of enthusiasm for the future of mankind.

GORDON BELL is Chief Technical Officer of Encore Computer Corporation which he joined in July of 1983. There he is responsible for Encore's technical excellence and overall product strategy. He is also dedicated to and responsible for providing industry, standard compatible products that work together.
Prior to joining Encore Computer, Dr. Bell was Vice President, Engineering, for Digital Equipment Corporation, with responsibility for the company's research, design and development activities in computer hardware, software, and systems. He also was a member of the Operations Committee, Digital's senior management team.

Bell joined Digital in 1960 as Manager of Computer Design, a position he held for six years with responsibility for DEC's PDP-4, -5, and -6 computers. He took a leave of absence from Digital in 1966 to join the faculty of Carnegie Mellon University. As a consultant for Digital, 1966–1972 while at CMU, he worked on various computers and products including the PDP-11. He rejoined the company in 1972 as Vice President of Engineering.

Bell earned his B.S. and M.S. degrees in Electrical Engineering at Massachusetts Institute of Technology in 1956 and 1957, respectively, and held several engineering positions including that of research engineer at the MIT Speech Communications and Electronic Systems Laboratories prior to joining Digital.

He is a widely published author on computer architecture, and computer design. His books include "Computer Structures," co-authored with Allen Newell; "Computer Structures" with Siewiorek and Newell; and Digital Press books, "Designing Computers and Digital Systems, Using PDP-16 Register Transfer Modules," with John Grason and Allen Newell; and "Computer Engineering: A DEC View of Hardware Systems Design," co-authored with J. Craig Mudge and John McNamara.

Holder of several patents in the computer and logical design areas, Bell has also served the U.S. Government as a member of various committees including the National Science Foundation, the Council for International Exchange of Scholars, and the National Research Council. He is an active member of the board of The Computer Museum.

Bell is a member of the National Academy of Engineering, a Fellow of the Institute of Electrical and Electronic Engineers, a Fellow of the American Association for the Advancement of Science for Computing Machinery, and is affiliated with a number of other professional organizations. Among his awards are the Mellon Award, the McDowell Award and the Eckert-Mauchly Award for contributions to computer design.

ROBERT SPINRAD considers himself a computer scientist even though that term was not much in vogue when he received his formal training at Columbia (B.S. and M.S.) and M.I.T. (Ph.D.). It was at Columbia, in 1953, that he built his first computer—a rather rudimentary device made of discarded telephone company relays. The next one, a more serious affair, was built in 1958 when he was a staff member at Brookhaven National Laboratory. He worked at Brookhaven until 1968 in a variety of positions, serving for the last few years as Senior Scientist and Head of the Computer Systems Group. In that role, he put the first computers on-line to experiments and led the development of the technique now known as laboratory automation. In 1968, Spinrad joined Scientific Data Systems, a small California computer company which, the following year, was acquired by the Xerox Corporation. He has been with Xerox ever since, serving through the years as Vice President of Programming, Director of Information Sciences, Vice President of Systems Development and Vice President of Research. His most recent role is as Corporate Director of Systems Technology. Spinrad keeps in touch with academia through his membership on numerous university visiting committees and research panels. His ruminations about the electronic university derive, in part, from his work at Xerox in office automation.

EDWARD E. DAVID, JR., engineer, research scientist, presidential advisor, private consultant, and business executive, has made many vital contributions in scientific research and technology. Born in North Carolina and educated at the Georgia Institute of Technology (B.S., 1945) and the Massachusetts Institute of Technology (S.M. and ScD., 1950), Dr. David has garnered many honors and awards for his civic and professional achievements over the past thirty years. President of the Exxon Research and Engineering Company since 1977, Dr. David has also served as Executive Director for Bell Laboratories' Research Communication Principles Division, a position which capped his productive twenty year career at Bell Laboratories. In 1970 he was appointed Science Advisor to the President and served as Director of the White House Office of Science and Technology (1970–1972). His active involvement with a number of organizations including the White House Science Council, the NATO Science Committee, the Executive Committee and Energy Science Advisory Board of MIT, and many others, reflect his concern for the contemporary challenges of science and society.

JOEL S. BIRNBAUM'S fascination and frustration with computers began when he was an engineering physics student at Cornell University in the late 1950's. This involvement deepened while he earned a doctorate in nuclear physics at Yale University; his thesis involved much computer-based data acquisition, analysis and display, but only the most flexible of his colleagues were enthusiastic about learning to use the complex new tools.

In 1965, Birnbaum joined IBM at the T.J. Watson Research Center in Yorktown Heights, N.Y., where he attempted to bridge the worlds of physics and computing by helping to design laboratory automation systems that offered many new capabilities while simplifying the routine tasks of the engineers and scientists. During the next fifteen years he was associated, first as a contributor, then as a manager, and finally as

Director of Computer Sciences, with a wide variety of systems and applications. The dual themes of making computers easier to use while improving their cost and performance were often present.

In 1980, he joined Hewlett-Packard Laboratories as Director of the new Computer Research Center, where he began extensive programs to develop the technologies necessary to produce a new generation of domesticated computers and to explore their application to fields as diverse as precision measurement instrumentation, office systems, computer-aided design, medicine and education.

In 1984, Birnbaum assumed his present position of Vice President and Director of HP Laboratories. He remains optimistic that computer technology will become generally useful before he becomes totally obsolescent technically.

PETER LIKINS is now President of Lehigh University, and he has served as Provost and earlier as Dean of Engineering and Applied Science at Columbia University, but he still regards university administration as an engaging distraction from the real work of the university: teaching and research. His student days at Stanford and MIT led to 12 years on the UCLA Faculty of Engineering and Applied Science, working on problems of dynamics and control with special application to spacecraft. Despite the current distractions, Dr. Likins continues his active interest in engineering research on such electromechanical systems as robots and spacecraft. He is a Fellow of the American Institute of Aeronautics and Astronautics and a member of the National Academy of Engineering. Dr. Likins is included in this volume as the creator of the Computer Science Department at Columbia University, which he initiated as Dean of Engineering and Applied Science and then nurtured as Provost. All credit for the success of the department he attributes to its members and founding chairman, Joe Traub.

LEWIS M. BRANSCOMB is a research physicist, corporate soothsayer and a central figure in national and international scientific and technological affairs. As vice president and chief scientist and a member of the Corporate Management Board at International Business Machines Corp., he is responsible for guiding IBM's scientific and technical programs to ensure that they meet long-term needs. Dr. Branscomb joined IBM in 1972 following a 21-year career at the National Bureau of Standards which was capped in 1969 by his appointment by the President as director of the NBS. A native of North Carolina, he is a graduate of Duke University and

Harvard, where he later taught and was elected this year to the Board of Overseers. Among his many professional affiliations, Dr. Branscomb has been a member of the President's Science Advisory Committee (1965–1968), the President's Commission for the Medal of Science (1970–1972) and the President's National Productivity Advisory Committee (1982–1983), and Chairman of the National Science Board (1980–1984), which is the policy-setting body for the National Science Foundation. Widely regarded as a lively and original thinker about science and technology, he is a frequent and forceful speaker on these subjects and their multi-faceted implications for society.

ARNO PENZIAS is Vice President of Research at AT&T Bell Laboratories. He began his scientific career in 1961 when he joined Bell Laboratories as a Member of Technical Staff. He conducted research in radio communication and related areas, and also took part in the pioneering Echo and Telstar communications satellite experiments. As a scientist, he is best known for his work in radio astronomy, especially his part in the discovery of evidence supporting the "big-bang" theory of the origin of the universe, work for which he shared the 1978 Nobel Prize for Physics. Over the years he has held a number of managerial positions in Bell Laboratories Research and was named to his present position as Vice President of that organization in December 1981. This responsibility covers a wide range of programs in the physical, material, communications and information sciences.

Dr. Penzias' current personal research includes the study of chemical molecules in outer space, with particular emphasis on how the elements in these molecules are formed. He maintains close ties with the academic community, having been a member of Princeton University's Astrophysical Sciences Department since 1967, where he regularly acts as thesis advisor to graduate students. He is also an adjunct professor of Earth and Space Science at the State University of New York at Stony Brook, as well as a member of the Board of Overseers of the School of Engineering and Applied Science, University of Pennsylvania.

Dr. Penzias received a Bachelor of Science degree in 1954 from the City College of New York. He served for two years as an officer in the U.S. Army Signal Corps, then attended Columbia University where he received his master's and doctorate degrees. He has received a number of honorary degrees and is the only American to hold an honorary doctorate from the Paris Observatory.

A member of the National Academy of Sciences, as well as a number of other scientific and professional organizations, Dr. Penzias is Chairman of the Editorial Committee of the *AT&T Bell Laboratories Technical Journal*, and a Vice Chairman of the Committee of Concerned Scientists, a national organization devoted to working for the political freedom of scientists in various countries.

 JOSEPH F. TRAUB is the Edwin Howard Armstrong Professor of Computer Science, Professor of Mathematics, and founding chairman of the Computer Science Department at Columbia University. He is Director of the New York State Center for Computers and Information Systems. Previously, he was head of the Computer Science Department at Carnegie-Mellon University. He has served as advisor or consultant to numerous organizations including Stanford University, IBM, Centre Mondial Informatique et Ressource Humaine, New York State Urban Development Corporation, Federal Judiciary Center, National Science Foundation, Hewlett-Packard, and Institut National de Recherche en Informatique et en Automatique. He is on the Board of Trustees of Columbia University Press.

In 1959, Professor Traub began his pioneering research in what is now called computational complexity. He has written some 80 papers and is author or editor of seven books. With his colleagues he is currently developing the field of information-based complexity. Its goal is to create a general theory about problems with limited or contaminated information, and to apply the results to solving specific problems in varied disciplines.

HERBERT A. SIMON, one of the founding fathers of artificial intelligence and cognitive science, has made research contributions to these fields for nearly thirty years. Educated in political science and economics at the University of Chicago (Ph.D., 1943), he has devoted himself to understanding how people make decisions, solve problems, and learn. Computer simulation of human thinking has served as his principal research tool.

After appointments at the University of California, Berkeley (1939–42), and Illinois Institute of Technology (1942–49), Professor Simon joined the faculty of Carnegie Institute of Technology (now Carnegie-Mellon University), where he is currently Richard King Mellon University Professor of Computer Science and Psychology. His research has won him many honors including the Distinguished Scientific Contribution Award of the American Psychological Association, the Allan Turing Award of the Association for Computing Machinery, the James Madison Award of the American Political Science Association, and the Alfred E. Nobel Memorial Prize in Economic Sciences.

He has been active in a wide range of public advisory functions, including service on the President's Science Advisory Committee (1968–72), the Chairmanship of the Board of the Social Science Research Council (1961–65), and membership on the Council of the National Academy of Sciences (1978–81, 1983–).

Index